Among the Sleeping Giants

Among the Sleeping Giants
Occasional Pieces on
Lewis and Clark

DONALD JACKSON
With a Foreword by Savoie Lottinville

University of Illinois Press URBANA AND CHICAGO

Also by Donald Jackson

Voyages of the Steamboat Yellow Stone (New York, 1985)

Valley Men: A Speculative Account of the Expedition of 1807 (New York, 1983)

Thomas Jefferson & the Stony Mountains: Exploring the West from Monticello (Urbana, 1981)

Letters of the Lewis and Clark Expedition: With Related Documents, 1783–1854. 2 vols. (editor, Urbana, 1978; first ed., 1962)

The Diaries of George Washington. 6 vols. (editor, with Dorothy Twohig, Charlottesville, 1976–79)

George Washington and the War of Independence (Richmond, 1976)

The Expeditions of John Charles Frémont, vols. 1 and 2 (editor, with Mary Lee Spence, Urbana, 1970–73)

Custer's Gold: The U.S. Cavalry Expedition of 1874 (New Haven, 1966)

The Journals of Zebulon Montgomery Pike: With Letters and Related Documents. 2 vols. (editor, Norman, Okla., 1966)

Black Hawk: An Autobiography (editor, Urbana, 1955)

© 1987 by the Board of Trustees of the University of Illinois
Manufactured in the United States of America
C 5 4 3 2 1

This book is printed on acid-free paper.

Library of Congress Cataloging-in-Publication Data

Jackson, Donald Dean, 1919–
    Among the sleeping giants.

    Bibliography: p.
    Includes index.
    1. Lewis and Clark Expedition (1804–1806)
    2. Lewis, Meriwether, 1774–1809. 3. Clark, William,
    1770–1838. 4. West (U.S.)—Description and travel—
    To 1848. 5. Jackson, Donald Dean, 1919– .
    I. Title.
    F592.7.J13 1987 917.8′042 87-5907
    ISBN 0-252-01467-7

For Mary Catherine

Contents

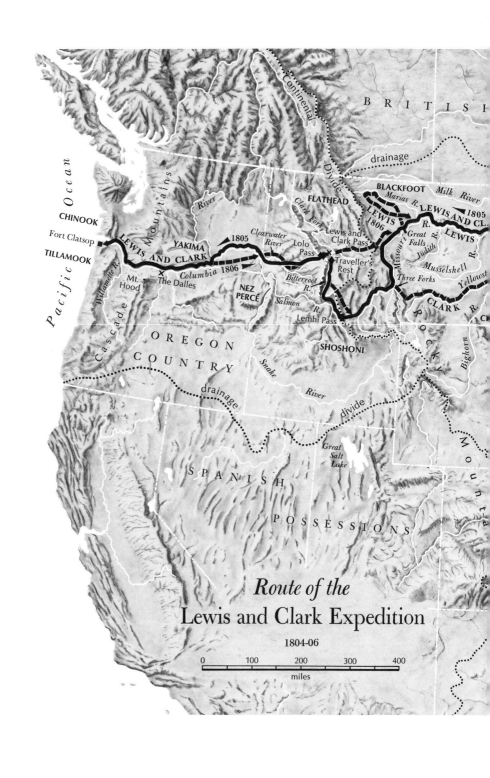

Route of the
Lewis and Clark Expedition

1804-06

0   100   200   300   400
miles

O S S E S S I O N S

divide

MINITARI

MANDAN

Fort
Mandan

1806

LEWIS AND CLARK

James

MISSOURI

R.

Little Missouri R.

Cheyenne

ARIKARA

TETON
SIOUX

RIVER

River

YANKTON
SIOUX

Niobrara R.

North

L O U I S I A N A

OMAHA

Platte River

South

OTO

LEWIS AND CLARK

1804

St.
Charles

St.
Louis

Lake Superior

Mississippi

River

Green Bay

INDIANA

Lake Michigan

Prairie du
Chien

TERRITORY

T E R R I T O R Y

Kaskaskia

MISSISSIPPI RIVER

Foreword

*T*he noble role of history in permitting us to look into the realities of the past is basic to the human records in the arts, sciences, law, medicine, theology, and, not least of all, exploration, the subject of Donald Jackson's newest book. How it leads into a discussion of a dog misnamed Scannon hangs upon its sometimes weakest link, curiosity, here directed to the epic experiences of the Lewis and Clark Expedition of 1803-6.

Curiosity, as a matter of fact, is its own reward. It needs no extended list of analogies of other dogs who merited a place in human history — from Argos in Homer's *Odyssey* to those depicted in other Greek and Roman histories, to the effigies of the Middle Ages, to the classic depictions in Renaissance paintings. Meriwether Lewis's black Newfoundland, in Jackson's mind, deserved a re-examination of his name, and with it a more secure place in the story of a great American adventure. His name turns out to be Seaman, in recognition of his fondness for salt or sweet waters, as a retriever of everything from ducks and geese to deer and beaver, taken by the expedition in the swift flow of western rivers.

The human interest such an episode evokes should be obvious, but as a lucid demonstration of the art of historical search-and-find it must also be highly rewarding, not only to general readers but to those who have pursued the Lewis and Clark journals and papers for the better part of two centuries. For in the misidentifications found there, Seaman was present all the while.

It withdraws nothing from the interest in this episode to say that it is but one of the unfoldings that Jackson has pursued for a lifetime, mainly in the collection and publication of historical documents clustered about Lewis and Clark, Thomas Jefferson, Black Hawk, Zebulon Montgomery Pike, John Charles Frémont, and George Washington, and narrative accounts of these historic figures and the eras in which they lived. If the United States has produced a premier editor of its historical documents, it seems to me he must be named Jackson.

But the exacting discipline imposed by the pursuit of past reality often leaves less than comfortable room for marginal detail, however attractive it may be. In Jackson's subtitle to this book, "Occasional Pieces on Lewis and Clark," he provides himself and us the desired saving grace. He finds room for a buffalo calf that, strangely, attaches himself to Joseph Field, out hunting from the exploring party at the mouth of the Yellowstone, and follows the explorer back to camp. And for the discovery of a hitherto undetected scientific anomaly, of geese on the Upper Missouri nesting in numbers in the abandoned aeries of eagles. Science had said these big birds were not arboreal. It had also not detected the insistence by magpies on nesting close to eagles.

Conjecture, which is supposed to be the enemy of sound history, has, however, a significant use in Jackson's consideration of what kind of result could have been expected if the Spaniards had intercepted Lewis and Clark somewhere on their route westward. Spain's forces were, indeed, to turn back the Freeman-Custis Expedition early in its progress up the Red River in 1806. A similar fate awaited Zebulon Montgomery Pike's thrust to the Conejos in southern Colorado late in February 1807, except that Pike would be marched off to Mexico. Spanish success in intercepting Lewis and Clark any time after 1804 could have aborted the U.S. tide of empire for decades.

The author has seized this opportunity to give us in short form a portrait of William Clark, fleshing out in human terms the historical figure who did a great deal more than survive the Lewis and Clark Expedition with distinction. It is a warm and understanding account of the governor of Missouri Territory, general of the Missouri Militia, and superintendent of Indian affairs at St. Louis, to his death in 1838. In it we are treated to the same richness of biographical quality that Jackson gave to his book-length treatment of Thomas Jefferson of half a dozen years ago.

Clark, whom many of us think of as the greatest cartographer of the early years of the republic, gave names to sites and physical features on the route to and from the Pacific, along with his co-commander, Lewis, and members of the expedition. Many, though not all, appear in Clark's maps, all of which, happily, we now possess either in original or faithful copy. One of the most rewarding features of Jackson's "Occasional Pieces" is the author's tracing of the survival rates for these Lewis and Clark names, directed mainly to what is now Montana. Many have disappeared from use, partly because they were undetected by others who came after the expedition had gone home (the first official record of the expedition, the Biddle text, did not appear until 1814, eight years after its return to St. Louis); partly because some have been corrupted in folk use; partly because many have vanished through displacement.

Jackson's research gives us 148 Lewis and Clark names for Montana, 20 of them of Indian origin. Of the 128 remaining, only 17 are in use today. A metaphorical delight lightens the burden of these disappearances: Grog Springs exists below Great Falls, at Cracon-du-Nez, a narrow strip of land separating the Teton and Missouri rivers by less than a hundred yards, hence the Nose Drip dreamed up by some nameless French-speaking namer of long ago.

Among the survivors are a number of robust ones translated by Lewis and Clark from Indian names: the Big Horn, the Musselshell, Beaverhead Valley, and Great Falls. Those that have stuck from the party's original namings include the Madison, Jefferson, Gallatin, and Judith rivers, to be joined with their translation of the earlier French Rivière des Roches Jaunes to Yellowstone River.

In any formal assessment of the work of a historian of the first class, the normal preoccupation of professionals is with concepts, leaving unsaid what is of underlying importance to grand designs, namely bibliography and its scientific management. Thus, for professionals and laymen alike, our attention is drawn to Tacitus and scarcely at all to Polybius; to Leopold von Ranke's *"wie es eigentlich gewesen,"* misinterpreting his meaning and overlooking his startling skills with sources; to Frederick Jackson Turner's concept of the frontier in U.S. development, leaving uncelebrated Charles C. Royce's *Land Cessions in the United States*.

As I have tried to indicate in *The Rhetoric of History,* Donald Jackson has been offering us correctives which few can deny he has achieved with remarkable success. Of all his works, perhaps the most compact group demonstrating his command of method in the editing of historical documents and, indirectly, in the construction of narrative history are, first, *Letters of the Lewis and Clark Expedition: With Related Documents, 1783-1854* (1962); second, in a classic essay, "Some Advice for the Next Editor of Lewis and Clark" (*Bulletin of the Missouri Historical Society,* 24:1, 52-62); and now, in more extended form, his next to last essay in the present volume, "Editing the Letters of the Lewis and Clark Expedition."

Here, in these writings, everything comes together. The dichotomies I have described go away. With singular fidelity, Thomas Jefferson's two captains of discovery are shown to have adhered religiously to his instructions. Animal, avian, and plant species are quickly introduced into our developing taxonomic consciousness. The work of our heroic map-maker, William Clark, is advanced from St. Louis to the far Pacific. When the captains stumble over their own transliterations of Indian and tribal names, the editor makes everything straight in concisely stated annotations.

And with it all, Jackson has had the good taste to spare general readers of the present volume the burden of scholarly apparatus, however greatly he has given order to and simplified the latter in many other works, for present and future generations. The National Archives and Records Service, the University of Illinois, the University of Virginia, the University of Oklahoma, the American Philosophical Society, and many other learned bodies, as well as the general public, can be grateful for his bright emergence among us.

That said, he was an editor-publisher at the University of Illinois Press for much of his professional career, while I was doing the same at the University of Oklahoma Press. Thus, the secret is out: the cloth binding for his splendid two volumes (boxed) of *The Journals of Zebulon Montgomery Pike: With Letters and Related Documents* is not mere buckram: it's linen, the stuff of immortality.

Savoie Lottinville

Really, there ought not to be a State, a City,
a Promontory, a River, an Harbor, an Inlett,
or a Mountain in all America, but what should be
intimately known to every Youth, who has any
Pretensions to liberal Education.

—John Adams to Abigail Adams, 13 August 1776

At the Mouth of the Yellowstone: An Introduction

*T*hink of it: freezing weather the last week of April. The men of the expedition backed out of their buffalo robes, stepped into the morning air, and knew that their tents would have to be struck and packed with cold, stiffening fingers.

They had spent the night at a wooded point on a bend of the Missouri River, not far below the mouth of the Yellowstone. It was a triumph of sorts to have come so far, these Americans from Virginia, Kentucky, and a few other states back home. In this year of 1805 no white man was known, at least to these travelers, to have come so high up the Missouri as to approach the Yellowstone.

So this morning's hasty meal would be a kind of victory breakfast; no ham and fried eggs for these men of the South with plantation appetites, but maybe grits with a drizzle of hot grease and a slab of buffalo hump from yesterday's kill. They would eat standing, shivering, and the first ones finished would warm themselves by repacking the cottonwood dugouts that were pulled up on the sand where the group had camped.

The men were two dozen soldiers, some recruited especially for this mission, and others, already in uniform, now detached from their regular units. Chosen for their woodsmanship and other skills, they included such specialists as a blacksmith, gunsmith, carpenter, tailor, and hunters, all keen of eye and not easily winded at the oars. Rounding out the party were a couple of interpreters and guides, a teenaged Shoshoni girl with a tiny baby, a slave named York, and an ebullient Newfoundland dog named Seaman who had just shown his independence by staying out all night.

Their leaders, as the whole world would know if they survived and returned, were captains Meriwether Lewis and William Clark.

Early on 25 April, they shoved the cottonwood boats back into the water. A red one and a white one, larger than the others, were called pirogues by French and American settlers, and the six smaller ones were just plain dugout canoes. The larger would accommodate six or seven men at the oars plus some equipage, and each boat was supplied with a square sail for those rare and lucky times when the wind was fair. All the craft had been caulked and pitched to fill the long cracks that had formed in the wind-shaken trunks.

This morning the wind had come up so briskly from the north that sailing was out of the question and even rowing was going to be difficult. When the dripping oars were lifted as the men strove to propel the little fleet upstream, a glister of ice shone on the blades. The river was so crooked that hoisting the sails was futile, for no reach of water ahead promised to allow more than three miles of fair wind.

After a morning of slow going, the captains talked it over. At this rate the expedition would have to camp at least one more night before reaching the Yellowstone, but a party on foot could cut overland and reach it today. If Lewis were to take a few men and go ashore on the south side, he could save some time for making astronomical observations while the boats were inching up to meet him.

Lewis picked four men, distributing the camping and surveying gear among them, and at eleven o'clock they jumped ashore when their pirogue bumped the bank, the wind from starboard helping the steersmen to hold the craft against the willow-fringed shore. They made their way through the flats of greening willows, then plunged into the cottonwoods on slightly higher ground, until they reached the foot of a bluff that Lewis hoped would lead them west to the mouth of the Yellowstone.

His companions included the two Field brothers, Joseph and Reubin from the knobby lands along the Salt River in Kentucky, and both as deadly with their rifles as all Kentuckians were believed to be. Also in the party was George Drouillard, a civilian hunter and all-round stalwart hired at Fort Massac on the Ohio, and one of Lewis's wisest choices for the expedition. The fourth man was Sergeant John Ordway, equally dependable and one of the few who could write well enough to keep a journal of the voyage.

And there was Seaman, the dog that Lewis had bought for twenty dollars along the wharves of Philadelphia or in the shipyards of Pittsburgh. Seaman was a bold and tireless companion who loved the water but agonized when prickly pear spines lodged in the pads of his feet.

The Yellowstone or Yellow Stone was the second fabled and mysterious, uncharted river along the Lewis and Clark route—the Platte having been the first. Europeans called it the Roches Jaunes or Rio de Amarillo and pondered on its sources. There was a "height of land" image of the inner continent that made sense to mapmakers: somewhere in the vastness of the West was an area where all the great western rivers were generated. The Missouri, Yellowstone, and Platte flowed eastward; the great Columbia or Oregon coursed westward to the Pacific; the Rio del Norte or Rio Grande ran south to something vaguely known as the Gulph of California. To test this theory, and also the theory that there was a water passage or short portage which might open the continent to trade and travel, was the principal goal of the Lewis and Clark Expedition.

After walking about four miles, the high sun reminding them that breakfast had been eaten just after dawn, the hikers killed a yearling buffalo calf at the foot of the bluff, dined on veal, and proceeded. Everyone kept an eye out for Indians. Although they were to see plenty of evidence—abandoned temporary shelters, hunting camps, sweat lodges— they were to see no tribes as they traversed the long stretch of the Missouri that lay between them and the Continental Divide.

The long bluff was multicolored, as if molded of gray putty with dabs of ochre and cadmium yellow worked in. It appeared to have been positioned by nature to keep the Yellowstone from meandering too widely as it snaked in to join the Missouri. Ahead, as Lewis and his men hiked along, the bluff seemed to turn southward and drop from sight. They decided to start climbing for a clearer view of the valley.

When they had gone about eight miles, Lewis led them up what he called the "river hills." To see a fertile valley, after the sparse lands they had been passing through, was exciting. This is how Lewis remembered it when he wrote of it in his journal: "I had a most pleasing view of the country, particularly of the wide and fertile vallies formed by the missouri and the yellowstone rivers, which occasionally unmasked by the wood on their borders disclose their meanderings for many miles in their passage through these delightfull tracts of country." The confluence of the rivers was hidden by trees, but Lewis knew it was close at hand. He decided to camp by the river at the closest place he could see, about two miles away. "The whole face of the country was covered with herds of Buffaloe, Elk & Antelopes . . . so gentle that we pass near them while feeding, without appearing to excite any alarm among them."

They killed three buffalo cows and a calf but the meat of two cows was tough, so they dressed the more edible one and hung the meat out of the reach of wolves, saving the calf carcass and some marrow bones for immediate use. Lewis shot a nesting goose and obtained six eggs from her nest. Two miles from the river's mouth they found a place to camp, and at sundown the wind died.

The next morning, as Lewis was setting up his equipment for a day of

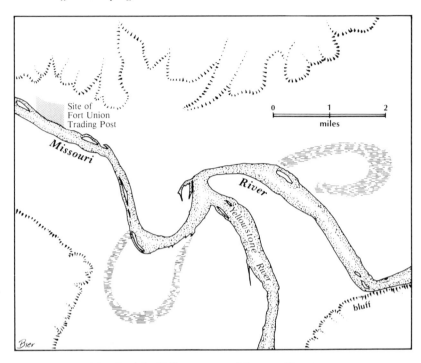

Mouth of the Yellowstone and Surrounding Area

observations that would fix the latitude and longitude when the proper formula was applied, he sent Joseph Field up the Yellowstone for a look around. Two others went back for the meat they had hung, and another wandered downstream to inspect the confluence.

Sergeant Ordway's journal provides a diversion. A herd of antelope (later to be called pronghorns by naturalists) got caught in midstream while swimming the river, and the alert Newfoundland splashed in after them, overtaking one laggard animal. "Drowned & killed it and Swam to Shore with it."

Lewis rose early and tried to get a longitude reading from the position of the moon and the star Aquilae, but the skies clouded over and he decided not to try for longitude at this place. He took a reading of the sun at nine o'clock and would match it in midafternoon with another reading to obtain a pair of equal altitudes. He would also take a reading at high noon, or as close as he could come by judging the shadows and relying cautiously on the chronometer that had been allowed to run down and was therefore suspect. The time was not so important in determining latitude, but for longitude it was critical. Lewis would have been correct in suspecting that the most reliable mapping technique the expedition had available was Clark's dead reckoning, done by patiently recording the compass headings and estimating the distance traveled. Clark was best at that, and in fact he was the expedition's mapmaker, a skill he had learned through years of surveying Kentucky and Virginia frontier lands.

The fact that Lewis observed the sun and moon through a new sextant of shining brass, while Clark guessed expertly at distances and never let his simple, pocket-worn compass get far out of reach, was only one of the differences between the two leaders. Lewis might have thought of a dozen more, as he sat in the spring sun by the riverside and waited to make his next reading. Lewis was in military terms the official leader of the command, with a captain's rank; Clark had been denied equal rank through bureaucratic obdurance and was only a second lieutenant, although he had been captain of a rifle company under General Anthony Wayne during the Indian Wars. The enlisted men were never told of this inequity. Lewis was a climber of hilltops, alone and pensive; Clark stuck with the men and saw to the details. When Thomas Jefferson had conceived the expedition in 1802, Lewis was the President's aide and a familiar figure in the legislative halls and ballrooms of Washington; Clark was looking after the affairs of older brother General George Rogers Clark, and doing so-so as a country squire in the neighborhood of Louisville.

Lewis himself had concealed Clark's lesser rank and insisted that the two were co-leaders in every way. He would have been the first to admit that as he sat there with a gadget that he knew little about, making readings of doubtful accuracy despite some special training in Philadelphia, Clark was leading the men most ably, and together they made a splendid team. Perhaps the mercurial Lewis, melancholic and often indecisive, a born worrier, fully realized how much he needed the steadying hand and practical turn of mind that he had found in William Clark.

The day passed placidly for Lewis, who fished for a while and observed the landscape for a journal entry. He thought he was seeing more timber than he had encountered since passing the mouth of the Cheyenne. Cottonwood, mostly, with some white elm, green ash, and box elder. On the sandbars and along the "verge of the river" he found a small-leaved willow; in the lowlands, a different willow and wild roses that stood three or four feet high and still bore bright red berries or hips carried over from last fall. He saw serviceberry and redbud, gooseberry and chokecherrry, currant, and—on drier ground—a kind of artemisia that he called wild hysop.

At about noon, perhaps while he was taking his second reading of the sun, he heard gunfire from downstream that told him the boats had arrived. He sent Drouillard to bring up one of the small dugouts and retrieve the meat his men had hung the night before.

Late in the afternoon, Joseph Field came in from his excursion up the Yellowstone. He had gone about eight miles as the crow flies, he said, and had found a stream coming in from the southeast. A buffalo calf had followed him back and would stick with him until the party was united that evening. Perhaps the biggest piece of news Field had was his sighting of a bighorn sheep. Lewis and Clark had learned of the animal back at the Mandan villages during their winter months there, and had sent horn specimens home to Thomas Jefferson, but as yet no living bighorns had been seen. Although Private Field had been unable to get close enough for a shot, he had brought in a recurved and serrated horn he had picked up to prove his claim. Thus the creature they would at first call an ibex or argali was added to their growing list of natural history specimens. Besides scores of new botanical finds, Lewis and Clark had described or collected the antelope or pronghorn, coyote, jackrabbit, prairie dog, blacktailed deer, and a respectable list of new birds.

Near sundown, when Lewis's party gathered their gear and strolled down to where Clark had made camp on a point of land at the confluence, there undoubtedly was meat browning on a spit, tents staked out on dry ground, and logs being dragged in for firewood and seats beside the campfire. It had been a satisfying day for the whole expedition.

After Lewis and the others had gone ashore, Clark kept the boats well out of the channel where the water was easier on the men rowing. All seemed well aboard the little fleet; some of the men, not assigned to the oars, were coddling a litter of wolf cubs they had taken the day before. But rowing with the bitter wind sometimes abeam, sometimes meeting them head on, was not getting them upstream. Gritty squalls of gray sand peppered their eyes and seemed intent on blasting the paint off the pirogues. So Clark pulled the flotilla ashore to wait for more favorable conditions.

The men were free to go ashore and seek shelter from the wind, as was Sacagawea and the baby, whose head she had swathed in a blanket. Perhaps she sat on a shard of driftwood with her back to the wind and hummed Shoshoni music into the folds of the tiny bundle.

Clark had noticed something curious about the geese they had been killing for meat and eggs. These birds liked to nest in abandoned eagle aeries at the tops of dead cottonwoods. It was a phenomenon that he would record in his journal, and one that later observers would puzzle over for generations; the common belief back home was that geese always nested on the ground. Clark also noticed that magpies, hitherto unreported in North America until he and Lewis had encountered them the previous fall, seemed eager to nest as close to the eagles as possible.

At about five o'clock in the afternoon the wind subsided and Clark, unwilling that the day should be a total loss, headed the boats upstream so that he could log a few more miles. They camped, and that night Clark tallied up his courses and distances for the day. They had made eight course changes and had come only about fourteen miles.

On the morning of 26 April they set out in freezing weather. Having nothing physical to do to keep him warm, Clark went ashore to walk along the bank. He would go aboard again when the sun began to warm the back of his neck. He noticed that the river had risen three inches overnight.

To the crew in the boats he was an army captain, and that was important in maintaining his authority. What hurt, though, was the realization that he was not a captain in the eyes of Thomas Jefferson, Secretary of War Henry Dearborn, or members of the Senate who would have needed to provide the "advice and consent" to confirm his commission. The thought rankled in a way he could never fully reveal.

It must have been hard for Clark, a loyal Jeffersonian Republican, to accept the fact that the President had hampered his commissioning by inattention. Lewis had written an offer that spelled out the terms: "He [Jefferson] has authorized me to say that in the event of your accepting this proposition he will grant you a Captain's commission which will of course intitle you to the pay and emoluments attached to that office." But the actual granting of a commission was not in Jefferson's hands; somewhere in the bureaucracy his rank had been changed from captain in the Corps of Engineers to second lieutenant in the Corps of Artillerists. The helpless Lewis, as angry as Clark, could only swear that the emoluments would be the same, and that the members of the expedition were not to know. When it was necessary for Clark to sign a voucher or other paper bearing his name and rank, he called himself captain of a Northwest Corps of Discovery.

So here he was, thrashing about in the willows on the Upper Missouri, not even aware that some day the trip would be known as the Lewis and Clark Expedition. As of now it was his friend Lewis's undertaking and he was second in command, authorized by Jefferson to take charge if something happened to Lewis. The journey was going to be a test of loyalty as well as skill and, Clark might well have supposed, a long exposure to the whims of chance.

He noted an abundance of beaver and thought they were larger than those he had seen downstream. One of the rascals had felled a cottonwood nearly three feet across. He shot a beaver and two deer as his day's contribution to the larder.

Clark's first glimpse of the Yellowstone was in such contrast to Lewis's that it might have served to remind him once again of his equal-but-secondary status. Lewis had seen the confluence from the heights, enjoying a grand view of the whole valley; Clark, squinting across the gray-white water from the bow of a pirogue, first noticed the point of land at the confluence—where tonight's campsite would be—and could not have distinguished it from most of the large islands they had approached in recent days. Only a slight difference in the hue of the Yellowstone water, as it surged in to join that of the Missouri, told him that another blank space on his map was about to fill up.

Clark occupied himself with miscellaneous observations while waiting for Lewis's party to come in. He calculated the width of the Yellowstone at 297 yards, the odd number indicating that he actually made a measurement instead of an estimate. He may have used a simple geometric procedure: treating the width of the river as the leg of a triangle, after marking off an identical triangle along the shore with a surveyor's chain and a plane-table sighting. At this time the Yellowstone was falling and the Missouri rising, he noted in his journal. "At our arrival at the forks," he wrote, "I observed a Drove of Buffalow Cows & Calves on a sand bar in the point. I directed the men to kill the fattest Cow, and 3 or 4 calves, which they did and let the others pass, the cows are poor, [the] calves fine veele."

A gill of "ardent spirits" was four fluid ounces, the army's official ration for a day. It could make you glow inside if you had been without a drink for some time, especially when the liquor consisted of concentrated brandy to allow more alcohol per keg. That night, with the two parties united and everyone in a glowing mood, Lewis and Clark decided that a gill all around was called for.

Before the captains could relax with a dram, there were journal entries to write. "The Indians inform," Lewis wrote, "that the Yellowstone river is navigable for perogues and canoes nearly to it's source in the Rocky Mountains, and that in it's course near these mountains it passes within less than half a day's march of a navigable part of the Missouri. It's extreem sources are adjacent to those of the Missouri, river Platte, and I think probably with some of the south branch of the Columbia river." His Indian informants, probably the Hidatsas who lived downstream near the Mandans, had told him what they knew, or what some interpreter thought they knew. Later the expedition would discover that the part about the Yellowstone being half a day's march from the Missouri was wrong. The other misstatement, about the sources of the rivers, conformed to information or conjecture that was part of Lewis's mental baggage.

Clark wrote, among other things, of a small lake the men had discovered not far from the point upon which they had camped. It probably was an old oxbow that the river had cut off and moved away from.

The travelers were as close to merriment as any party of wayfarers facing the unknown could have been. At various times on the expedition, Pierre Cruzatte could be expected to break out his fiddle and play French folk tunes and no doubt an American melody or two. He did that tonight, one-eyed Cruzatte the halfblood Indian, temporarily a private in the army, serving the group as a hunter and guide. His notoriety in history was not to come from violin music, however, but from his error on the trip home from the Pacific in mistaking Lewis for an elk in the underbrush and seriously wounding him in the backside.

Some perverse urge in the modern historian makes him want to call back through time and tell these people what lies ahead, even if the news is somber. He calls in vain, but let him try:

Yes, Lewis and Clark, you will make it to the great ocean and return home heroes. Starvation, dangers, uncertainties lie ahead but will not deter you. But there are worse things to tell you and your detachment.

Meriwether Lewis, you will be dead by your own hand within less than five years. Not what the American people expect of their heroes.

William Clark, the western tribes will come to love you when you become their agent and representative in St. Louis, but by the end of your faithful service to them in 1838 the temper of the times will have overrun you, and the tribes, and destroyed Jefferson's dream of an orderly assimilation of the Indians into the new American family.

Sacagawea, your role is to become a legend in the folklore of another race, even as your own life as one of old Charbonneau's wives ends in 1812. By then you will know that the baby, little Jean Baptiste, will be raised and educated by that good man William Clark.

Charbonneau, you rascal, of little use to the expedition except as spouse to the Indian girl, you will live out your life among the Mandans, officially an interpreter employed by the U.S. government.

York, black servant to Clark—you will learn that following your master across the Rocky Mountains and back makes you a well-known personage but a slave and a black man still.

John Colter, George Drouillard, John Potts—look well upon the Yellowstone waters, for they will lure you back to beaver country, which is, unhappily, also Blackfoot Indian country. Potts, you will die there, but Colter will discover such wonders at the head of the river that men will smile in disbelief when you spin the tale.

George Shannon, future student at Transylvania University, then attorney and judge—you will lose a leg on a mission for Captain Lewis after this adventure, but still become a star alumnus among the enlisted men of the expedition.

Nathaniel Pryor, congratulations on your appointment to a commission as ensign after the expedition. Too bad your promising military career will be brief and your remaining life as a trader one of hardship and struggle.

Joseph and Reubin Field, back to the Kentucky hills for you—lost to history.

Patrick Gass, you will be the first to publish a journal, with the vitality edited out of it by your Pittsburgh publisher. It will predate the official account of the expedition by seven years.

Robert Frazer, your journal, the one you advertised in the newspapers along with a great map of the West—whatever happened to it? Nobody published it, nobody has found it.

Joseph Whitehouse, your often clumsy journal will come to light and give us many new details of the expedition. Thank you for your doggedness.

Bratton, Collins, Gibson, Hall, Howard, McNeal, Shields, Thompson, Warner, Windsor—drain your ardent spirits, put your hands to the oars tomorrow, and forget about fame. You will be names only, accompanied by brief snippets of biographical data in the pantheon of American explorers.

Tomorrow the expedition will be on its way. The captains will find a site a few miles up the Missouri which they will recommend to Jefferson as a strategic location for a fort and government trading house (but Fort Union will first be a private trading post, and not a military fort for another generation). Then onward they will go, across what will one day become Montana, Idaho, Washington, and Oregon, portaging the Great Falls, struggling across the tremendous sierra that Jefferson calls the Stony Mountains, and down roaring watercourses to the Pacific.

But tonight the fiddle plays, the baby cries, the men cup their stiff and calloused hands around the brandy, and the campfire sinks into golden coals.

If the Spaniards had Captured
Lewis and Clark

*A*rtists sketch idly on grassy hillsides, unconcerned if some of their charcoal productions do not prove to be "keepers." Woodwind players stand by open windows in springtime, running chromatic scales and rehearsing sustained tones. Surgeons are said to practice tying knots in catgut with one hand. Pilots flying over the Sierra Nevada continually quiz themselves on where they will try to set the plane down if something goes amiss.

Historians also have a few ways of keeping in trim, and one is to play the old "what if" game. What if the South had won the Civil War? What if France had not come to the aid of the American colonists during the American Revolution, and the British had retained control of North America? It is easy to include Lewis and Clark in this kind of diversion. Seldom has an event in history been swung so easily in this or that direction by the winds of chance, and the decisions of a small band of men who barely knew where they were and what lay beyond the next ridge. And the game goes like this:

What if the Spaniards had captured Lewis and Clark?

It might have been high drama, had not fate so poorly organized the scenes. The main characters were separated by oceans, deserts, and mountains, and the lines they intoned were separated by weeks and months of pauses. Only in retrospect do the parts coalesce and become real theater.

In the United States, President Jefferson and his secretary of state, James Madison, sat in Washington and the minister from the court of Spain held forth in Philadelphia. A special Spanish envoy lived in New Orleans, sending urgent messages to his superiors in the court of Spain and to the commanding general of "New Spain" in Chihuahua. The principal subject of their communications was the aftermath of the purchase in 1803 of the Louisiana Territory, which France had sold to the United States. Spain—the former owner—was being testy about the sale for what it considered valid reasons. Both Spain and the United States were in a fog about the actual boundaries. A sensitive area was the mouth of the Mississippi, which was inner America's outlet to the sea. But the western and southwestern boundaries, shown on no authentic map and described in inexact language in the purchase documents, were equally important and subject to examination. For now, the Spanish considered them forbidden territory to U.S. adventurers and explorers.

Even before Lewis and Clark had reached the Mississippi, in the fall of 1804, Jefferson had appointed James Monroe as a special envoy to the court of Spain, to negotiate the boundaries and induce Spain to give up her claim to East and West Florida, removing her pincer-grip on the outlet of the Mississippi to the sea. The alternative to Monroe's successful negotiation might be war. Many a western settler, some conniving land speculators, and a few conspirators such as Aaron Burr and his confidantes, would have welcomed a war that gave them a reason to invade Mexico or separate some of the indecisive western states from the Union, or both.

Monroe's mission failed in all respects. The Spaniards were being hard-nosed and confident that the United States would not push its demands too far. The disappointed Monroe advised that the Americans take possession of the Floridas and the whole of the Louisiana Purchase as far as the Rio Grande River.

In the midst of all this contention, these dashed hopes, Jefferson sent Lewis and Clark off into territory claimed by Spain. Once they left St. Louis in May 1804, he was not to hear from them by messenger for a year, and then not for eighteen more months before they returned to St. Louis. Eager to learn what he could about the newly acquired Purchase, Jefferson was to send two expeditions on his own and approve the sending of another. Thomas Freeman's party was stopped on the Red River in 1806 and sent packing by the Spanish. Zebulon Pike—dispatched by the commanding general of the U.S. army—was arrested on the Rio Grande in early 1807, held prisoner in Mexico, and sent home with many a Spanish protest about his incursion. But the first of the expeditions to be sought after, the one the Spaniards wanted the most and tried perhaps four times to intercept, was that of Lewis and Clark.

The sparseness of communication lines and the tardiness of messengers hampered the Spaniards. General Nemesio Salcedo, in charge of the Spanish provinces from his headquarters in Chihuahua, learned of the Lewis and Clark Expedition by June 1804, when the captains were already approaching the mouth of the Kansas River. In August, when he dispatched a party of Indians and citizens commanded by Pedro Vial to find and capture Lewis and Clark, the expedition was well above the mouth of the Platte. Vial's party journeyed northeastward from Santa Fe to the villages of the Pawnee Indians along the Platte, gathered what information they could, apparently concluded they were too far behind Lewis and Clark, and started for home 20 September. Their quarry had made it to the Upper Missouri and was beyond capture.

One of the reports passed along by word of mouth, when Lewis and Clark were far above the Mandan villages, told of their interception by the Spaniards. It was stale news when it reached Jefferson, and he was canny enough to dismiss it as grapevine rumor.

But suppose the news had been genuine, contained in a letter from the Spanish chargé d'affaires in Philadelphia, with a copy to His Most Catholic Majesty in Spain, and suppose it told of a clash of arms between Vial's motley posse and the Lewis and Clark voyagers. Unknown fatalities, unknown casualties; the expedition broken and Spanish pride validated.

Now for the speculation. What would Jefferson and the nation have done if word had come back that Lewis, the President's private secretary and close friend, and William Clark, from one of the most respected families in Kentucky, had been slain, wounded, or even just manhandled and imprisoned by a Spanish force?

Ordinarily level-headed, Jefferson was capable of abandoning control — as he did later when he toyed with the use of extralegal means to convict Aaron Burr. Already believing that one day the entire northern and southern hemispheres would be free of Spanish domination, and suspecting that war with Spain was probable within a few years, Jefferson might well have lost his composure and taken immediate action. Westerners already impatient with the "dons," and eager to expand onto new lands and perhaps take possession of Mexico, might have found the President and Congress willing to see it happen.

Americans might not have waited until 1819 to negotiate a southwestern boundary with Spain, or until 1846 to march on Matamoros and occupy California. There might never have been an independent Republic of Texas. Cuba, which Jefferson thought should be an outer bastion of American defenses, might have fallen. It is conceivable that the interests of the United States might have jibed with those of Simón Bolívar, who was attempting to liberate South America, and a coalition with Bolívar could have crushed Spanish control of the hemispheres forever.

The "what if" game is more fun if played audaciously.

What if gold had been discovered at Willard's Creek?

The history of the American West seems so tied to the concept of gold rushes—in California, Nevada, Alaska—that it is strange to contemplate a time when men were not crouched in stream beds with their panning outfits, or swinging picks and shovels in hard-fought-for diggings. Yet, as if a virulent land fever were stimulating enough for the first few generations of Americans, there was not much gold fever. Jefferson had little to say about precious metals in his wide-ranging *Notes on the State of Virginia*, published in the 1780s. By the end of that century it was known that gold could be found in the Appalachian piedmont of North Carolina, but not until the 1820s did something like gold-camp excitement develop there, and another decade would pass before a thirst for Georgia gold mining became a factor in the removal of the Cherokee Indians from their lands.

Writing his instructions to Lewis in 1803, Jefferson stressed the importance of reporting on mineral productions. He meant, however, those unglamorous minerals like lead, iron, and coal, considered valuable adjuncts to an agricultural economy.

The entries that Lewis and Clark wrote in their journals about minerals and other geological features were routine and unexciting. Clark wrote on 16 May 1804 that the party "Passed a remarkable Coal Hill on the Larboard side," and comments about coal continued. Salt licks and salt springs were noted. On 10 June, "a great quantity of Stone calculated for whetstone."

In the late summer of 1805, as the expedition approached the foothills of the Continental Divide, an encampment was made on a small creek entering the Beaverhead River in what is now Beaverhead County, Montana. It was named Willard's Creek to honor Alexander Willard, a private soldier with the expedition. Nothing remarkable happened. No men wandered off into the gravel beds of the creek and came running back shouting "Gold! Gold!" The discovery at that location was not to come for nearly sixty years, long after the big strike at Sutter's Mill in California that sent men surging westward overland, and by sea around the Cape of Good Hope in the 1840s. Long after the "Pikes Peak or Bust" strike in Colorado in the late 1850s.

In 1862, Willard's Creek was to be renamed Grasshopper Creek, and the valleys in Beaverhead country were to teem with miners and their entourages, bringing "civilization" to yet another region of the untamed West.

Would the course of empire have been altered if Lewis and Clark had brought back a handful of nuggets from the crystal shallows of Willard's Creek? These things might have happened:

Nomadic fur traders, blazing trails in the years immediately following Lewis and Clark, might have been joined by adventurous miners. The finding of shorter and easier trails, such as the route across South Pass in southern Wyoming, would have occurred earlier. The timetable for western settlement would surely have been advanced by a generation, and that peculiar American invention, Indian removal, would have become standard government policy much earlier in the area west of the Mississippi.

What if the captains had decided it was unwise to travel with a teenaged Shoshoni girl and her new baby?

Lewis and Clark hired the French interpreter, Charbonneau, while they were among the Mandans, and young Sacagawea came in the bargain. Another of the man's three wives might have been chosen, but this girl had been captured from the Shoshonis and her knowledge of the language might be useful. The only problem was that her baby had been born just two months earlier. Who can say if she had the choice of staying or going? She joined the expedition and won the admiration of the men. Her tangible contributions to the voyage were her language ability, her recognition of certain landmarks that helped to orient the captains, and the incredible coincidence that a principal warrior of the Shoshonis turned out to be her brother. The reunion expedited the purchase of badly needed horses from the Shoshonis. Lewis and Clark also believed that Sacagawea's presence helped to convince some Indians that the expedition was not a war party.

Had she not gone along, the journals would have contained fewer human touches. Clark called her "the squar" and mangled her name awesomely as he recorded the progress of the party, but the two respected each other. When there was desperate hunger, the young woman gave — tried to give — Clark a crust of bread that she had been saving for herself or her child. When the expedition was encamped near the Pacific Ocean, and word got out that a whale had washed up on the beach, a small party was chosen to go and see the creature. Sacagawea had the audacity to complain that she thought she was entitled to see it also. And she did.

It was Clark who took her boy Jean Baptiste to St. Louis for an education. The pioneers, the town builders who came after Lewis and Clark, put her statue in city parks and named motels and bars for her. Today she is revered by feminists, puzzled over by historians, and loved by everyone who gets involved with the Lewis and Clark legend.

What if Lewis and Clark had come home by sea?

Attempting to foresee all the contingencies, Jefferson asked himself what Lewis should do if he made a successful crossing of the continent but found it inadvisable to return overland, perhaps because of "dangers from the Indian inhabitants." In his instructions to Lewis he wrote, "Should you be of opinion that the return of your party by the way they went will be eminently dangerous, then ship the whole, & return by sea, by the way either of cape Horn, or the cape of Good Hope."

In any case, Lewis was to seek passage by ship for two of his most trusted men, who would bring home duplicate copies of the journals. To facilitate these arrangements with American or European ship captains, Jefferson wrote a letter of credit for the expedition to carry, promising repayment for any expenses incurred in such sea travel.

The explorers saw no ships on the Pacific coast, although there was evidence that vessels called regularly in the region around the mouth of the Columbia. The natives possessed a modest lexicon of useful English phrases, including "son of a bitch," and gave Clark the names of several traders who appeared from time to time by sea. An American sailor, John Rogers Jewitt, later stated that he was aboard a Boston vessel which, in the fall of 1805 and again in the spring of 1806, dropped anchor in the Columbia River estuary. The Indians, he said, displayed several medals received from Lewis and Clark.

The captains showed every intention of returning home by land, perhaps never giving a thought to the alternative. They designated men to boil sea water for salt and dry meat for the journey. They worked out a plan to expand their coverage of the continent by breaking the detachment into parties to examine areas not seen earlier. Eventually these parties were to rendezvous at the mouth of the Yellowstone and proceed to St. Louis in one group.

A trip home by sea would have deprived Jefferson and the American people of eyewitness reports on the Yellowstone, Bitterroot, and Marias rivers, and the topography of their watersheds. Each of these rivers was strategic for a different reason. The unknown Yellowstone was the gateway to a vast region thought to be the source of all the major western rivers. The Bitterroot could provide a shorter route than the one they had used coming out. The Marias, flowing from the north and northwest, might help in determining the northern boundary of the Purchase.

There would have been no skirmish with the small band of vagrant Piegan Blackfeet on a tributary of the Marias, resulting in the death of two Indians and—some historians claim—years of bitter feelings by the

Blackfeet toward the Americans. On the other hand, there would have been no peaceful visit with the Nez Perce at Camp Chopunnish, so helpful in establishing American relations with that tribe.

A devotee of Lewis and Clark trivia could compile a handsome list of additional events that would not have become part of the captains' story if they had come home by sea. The process helps to demonstrate the strain that the "what if" game can place on logic and credulity. For example:

Returning overland, the expedition was welcomed at the Mandan villages near present Bismarck, North Dakota, and a principal chief named Sheheke was persuaded to join the voyagers for a visit to President Jefferson and to see the marvels of American civilization. Sheheke was taken to Washington and other East Coast cities, then returned to St. Louis and Fort Belle Fontaine to await an escort back to his village. The first expedition attempting to return him was commanded by Nathaniel Pryor, and another member of the party was George Shannon, both Lewis and Clark alumni (Pryor had by then been commissioned an ensign). Shannon was to lose a leg as the result of an attack by the Arikaras during this foray.

Not until 1809 did the leaders of a trading party from St. Louis agree to take Sheheke along when they traveled up the Missouri in pursuit of beaver pelts and buffalo robes. This time the attempt was successful and Sheheke rejoined his people, but there was an unfortunate result. Lewis, as governor of the Louisiana Territory, had authorized the spending of $940 in government funds to cover the cost of Sheheke's travel. As time was short, he made the expenditure before getting permission from the Secretary of War in Washington, and the War Department refused to endorse his voucher; he was held personally responsible for the money.

Lewis's financial position in the summer of 1809 was already shaky. He had made investments to the extent of his credit, and word of his new difficulty brought a clamor from his lenders. He decided that he must travel personally to Washington to see if he could clear himself with the new Madison administration. It was on this trip by horseback, deep in the grip of an addiction, beset by problems with his governorship, and now staggered by a severe blow to his financial stability, that he apparently shot himself while passing along the Natchez Trace. Did the invitation he extended to Sheheke, three years earlier on the Upper Missouri, make all the difference?

What if Lewis had not become an alcoholic?

In the personal tragedy of Lewis's addiction and early death, the loss of his services to the nation after the expedition seems paramount. His administration as governor of the Louisiana Territory (1807–9) was not a distinguished one for, possibly because of what Jefferson euphemistically called "hypochrondriac affections," Lewis seemed unable to cope with the political factions, the free-wheeling operations of a territorial government on the frontier. He made enemies who were in a position to hurt him; he hurt himself by errors of omission and commission. His estrangement from Jefferson, after what has been called a father-son relationship, resulted in an almost complete cessation of correspondence that must have been painful to both men.

Suppose that instead of sinking into the befuddlement of the helpless drinker, Lewis had gone confidently to St. Louis and—to quote Jefferson's rosy appraisal of his tenure there—actually had governed with "even-handed justice" that established "a respect for his person & authority," and even "wore down animosities and reunited the citizens again into one family." In the tradition of America's military and other outdoor heroes (Jackson, Taylor, Grant, Eisenhower), Lewis might then have become governor of Missouri Territory when it was formed from the Louisiana Territory in 1813, or moved on at once to national office. He could have served well in the cabinet of President James Madison or become a senator or congressman representing western interests. Then, with the memory of his journey to the Pacific still in the public consciousness, he might have been selected instead of James Monroe to be the fourth president of the United States in 1817. With John Quincy Adams as his secretary of state, Lewis might have sent an annual message to Congress in 1823, prepared in heavy collaboration with Secretary Adams—declaring the doctrine that the American hemisphere was no longer subject to colonization by European powers.

Class assignment for tomorrow: write a two-page essay on the subject "The Lewis Doctrine—has it been a viable factor in world politics?"

What if Jefferson had carried out one of his many threats to resign permanently from public office?

Like many of his countrymen, including George Washington, Jefferson accepted public service partly out of a grudging fascination with it and partly out of the urge to serve. It was common for a man entering or re-entering public life to set forth all the reasons why his doing so would doubtless bring calamity, not just to himself and his family but to the entire country. As Jefferson said more than once, he would rather be sick at home than in fine fettle at the seat of government.

As a young man, Jefferson had sought and gained a seat in the Virginia Assembly, a public office not far from Monticello and not very arduous. As a result of that service he was named in 1775 to his first national position, a seat from Virginia in the Continental Congress. But in the following year, after being absent from his post for four months, he resigned from Congress to spend six years absent from the national scene. He returned to it only after his wife, Martha, died in 1782.

During that period he served for a time as Virginia's wartime governor, an unhappy decision that led to another resignation.

Perhaps his most decisive resignation occurred when he left the post of secretary of state under President Washington. He went home to Monticello at the end of 1793, announcing to the world that from then on he was going to be a farmer and only a farmer. Convincing himself, if not others, that his resolve was firm, he began to renovate his farmlands, to rebuild his mansion, and to avoid politics even to the extent of refusing to read a Philadelphia newspaper. But within three years he was allowing his name to be put forward as a presidential candidate, and his narrow loss to John Adams made him vice-president. In 1801 he was elected president, and among the achievements of his first term were the purchase of the Louisiana Territory and the dispatching of the Lewis and Clark Expedition.

Certainly the character of our national epic of exploration would have been far different had Jefferson not engineered it. Would there even have been a national endeavor to send a party of explorers to the Pacific? Already there were firm claims to the Northwest on the part of several nations. The Spaniards had been sailing the coast for years, as had the Russians. Alexander Mackenzie had crossed the continent for Great Britain, and Captain George Vancouver had sent a party a hundred miles up the Columbia, and had claimed territory for his country in the Northwest. Even the French had got a toe-hold, when a voyage commanded by Jean François de Lapérouse had laid claim to Lituya Bay in Alaska as a potential trading post. With all these conflicting claims, it was inevitable that possession of the Pacific Northwest would have to be negotiated.

All in good time, the Federalists might have said if they had won the election of 1801. They bitterly opposed the Louisiana Purchase and the Lewis and Clark Expedition. And if Jefferson's own party had won—the most likely candidate for president being James Madison—Jefferson's own hopes for westward expansion might have lagged for many years, because Madison had little understanding of things western.

But as for our two principals, Meriwether Lewis might well have opted for a career in the army, where Jefferson had found him, and Clark would surely have carved out a career and an estate in the rapidly developing Ohio River Valley.

What if we knew as much about Lewis and Clark as we know about Washington and Jefferson?

The lives and times of our Founding Fathers contain few blanks, perhaps because eager historians—amateur and professional—had begun to chronicle their days while they were still alive. In the case of Washington, for example, we have accounts ranging from the fanciful but basically informative effusions of Mason Weems to the meticulous (for his time) editing of Jared Sparks, then the comprehensive assembling of Washington's letters by John C. Fitzpatrick in the 1930s, and the definitive edition begun in the 1960s by Donald Jackson and continued by W. W. Abbot.

Much of what we do not know about Lewis and Clark is fascinating trivia, surprisingly elusive like the real name of Lewis's dog Seaman—not learned until 1985. But there is serious stuff to be unscrambled as well.

We do not know when the journals or diaries, as we know them today, were written. If we knew this for sure, we would better understand the misplaced passages, the duplications, the enigmas. A consensus now forming among historians is that these materials were mostly finished and copied into the famous red morocco notebooks before the explorers returned home.

We have no journal of Lewis for an important leg of his journey, from St. Louis to the Mandan villages in 1804. Students have rationalized about this puzzle, some satisfying themselves with the belief that Lewis put his information into the form of charts, descriptions of Indian tribes, and other data that has survived. The risk of declaring too emphatically that Lewis kept no journal during this period, and at certain other times during the expedition, lies in the possibility that his missing writings are moldering away in some attic and will come to light.

And what about the journals of the enlisted men? We have those of Sergeants Ordway, Gass, Floyd, and Private Whitehouse. Clark wrote that seven of the literate men were keeping journals.

Most historians now believe that Captain Lewis shot himself three years after the expedition. Nobody can ever be sure because there were no eyewitnesses.

We do not know what members of the expedition looked like except the two captains—who had portraits made—and Willard and Gass, who lived long enough to see the invention of photography. Many members of the expedition were still alive when, in the early 1840s, explorer John Charles Frémont took the first daguerreotype outfit into the West. We came that close to documenting the faces of the Lewis and Clark Expedition.

Now and then the captains wrote that they had lost some of their papers and collected specimens in the river, or through spoilage in caches. William Clark lived for thirty years after the expedition and nobody thought to set down his recollection of what items were not recovered.

How could we have lost track of so many dauntless men who were players in this great saga? Of some we know almost nothing beyond their roles in the expedition.

Any number can play

The "what if's" are endless. What if the explorers had made wrong decisions as to what streams to follow at the confluence of the Missouri and Marias, and at the Three Forks of the Missouri? (This one has been worn a bit threadbare by writers beginning with Bernard DeVoto.) What would have been the effect of future U.S. relations with the western Indians if the truculent Teton Sioux in present South Dakota had been more tough-minded than the captains, especially Clark, who drew his sword at the right moment and saved the day? And what if Clark had been a Harvard graduate? How much poorer the literature of exploration would have been if Clark had written rich, beautiful prose, impeccably spelled. Would the expedition hold as special a place in the hearts of Americans today had it not begun "under a jentle brease" and proceeded on toward those "stupendious mountains"?

Among the Sleeping Giants

*I*t was hardly likely, William Clark must have thought, that he would find what he was looking for. The expedition had spent its first summer on the Missouri, toiling through the shallows and dragging their boats across sandbars, slapping at mosquitoes and cursing the cactus spines that pierced their footgear. Now these men were spending a drizzly day in mid-September, halfway into what would later become the state of South Dakota, and Clark was looking for a volcano.

The words were clear on the manuscript map he was following: "Old volcano." And Jefferson's instructions were just as clear: he and Meriwether Lewis were to keep an eye out for "volcanic appearances." The explorers never felt foolish when following these instructions, for the land was new and nobody had read or thought more about it than Jefferson. For twenty years, long before he became president, Jefferson had been trying to send an expedition westward, and always he had clung to notions that many of his friends and foes in government thought were silly. There was a mountain of salt, miles and miles long, somewhere up the Missouri—or there might be. Possibly there were ancient animals long thought to be extinct: the mammoth, the giant sloth. And volcanoes, perhaps. It would not hurt to look.

They looked for lava and found pumice or "pumey stones," which might indeed be a kind of lava. Clark's journal mentioned it, along with coal banks, white clay that might be made into "Spanish whiting" for paints, and rock "well calculated for Grind Stones." Useful products all, but less so than the lead, silver, and even gold the expedition might discover, and far less dramatic than a volcano.

So today, with an unnamed member of the party, Clark spent the daylight hours looking for an old volcano that showed clearly on the old map attributed to John Evans and James Mackay. At day's end he had found nothing of that nature, but at the evening campfire was evidence of two unusual finds in the field of zoology. Clark had killed the expedition's first pronghorn or antelope, and Private John Shields had brought in a curious and leggy animal with long ears and the speed of light. A jackrabbit, later generations would call it; Sergeant Ordway's journal described it as being "of a different discription of any one ever yet seen in the States."

As for the antelope or "Buck Goat," Clark's journal called it "verry actively made, has only a pair of hoofs to each foot, his brains on the back of his head, his Norstrals large, his eyes like a Sheep." Clark wrote that the creature was like the "Gazella of Africa," perhaps an indication that he had been using the four-volume encyclopedia that made up a part of the Lewis and Clark traveling library.

As for the pumice, Jefferson himself had been skeptical that pieces of this substance reported along the Missouri before the expedition were indeed lava. When Lewis and Clark began to receive reports of the badlands farther west, where the very earth seemed to smolder and produce a porous and multicolored stone, they gave up hope of finding evidence of volcanoes. During the winter they were about to spend among the Mandans, Clark was to perform a convincing experiment by burning pumice and certain earths together in a charcoal-fueled fire, until the whole mass took on the appearance of lava. The explorers had as yet seen no real lava, no "volcanic appearances."

By October of 1805, Lewis and Clark had trekked across the High Plains, following the Missouri until its affluents had dwindled to montane streams. They had floundered in the cruel snows of the Bitterroots, known hunger and despair, and were now descending the Columbia River. The Cascade Range loomed ahead, and the ever-deepening waters gave promise that the explorers were nearing the Pacific.

It was a happier time than they had known in the Rockies. Strange Indian tribes befriended them and sold them dried fish and other foods, including the dogs they had learned to eat during leaner months. On 18 October, just below the confluence of the Snake and Columbia rivers, they saw what Clark described as "a mountain bearing S.W. conacal form covered with Snow." In his table of courses and distances covered that day, he added, "This we suppose to be Mt. St. Helens." It proved to be Mount Adams, but no matter; the expedition had at last linked up with the great naval voyages of Spain, Russia, and Great Britain, and the name Clark applied to this white cone on the horizon had been given it by Captain George Vancouver of the British navy in 1792. The Pacific Ocean was finally within reach.

Before leaving the United States, Meriwether Lewis had seen in Philadelphia a copy of Vancouver's *A Voyage of Discovery to the North Pacific*

Ocean, and had decided it was too heavy and expensive to purchase for the expedition. Instead he had traced what he thought were the pertinent sections of Vancouver's maps of the northern Pacific coast, and this information had been transferred on instructions from Jefferson to a large, inclusive map which the explorers were carrying. This map incorporated all the information that cartographers in the government judged to be valid, including three mountain peaks in the Cascade Range named Mount Hood, Mount St. Helens, and Mount Rainier. Mount Adams was omitted.

The towering cones, all the more imposing because they stood apart from one another and dominated the landscape, might have meant more to Lewis and Clark than mere landmarks of their journey, for they were dormant volcanoes.

Vancouver's report of his expedition would have told them little about the volcanic nature of these sleeping giants, but it could have helped them in other ways. The British captain had sent a detachment under Lieutenant William Broughton, to ascend the Columbia as far as practicable in a boat. His journal, included in the published volumes, covered more than a hundred miles of the lower Columbia, the very section that Lewis and Clark were about to traverse.

A week after seeing the peak that they mislabeled Mount Adams, they spied another giant white cone in the west, and gave it the new name of Falls Mountain. Only after the expedition would Clark, finally seeing the Vancouver publication, enter this note beside a point of rocks on one of his sketch maps: "From this rock a Mountain covered with Snow may be seen supposed to be the one Vancouvers Lieutt called Mount Hood." The only other peak of Vancouver's that Lewis and Clark were to mention, and probably to glimpse lying to the north, was Mount Rainier. They went into camp below the mouth of the Columbia, and spent a rainy winter among the Clatsop Indians writing their reports and planning their trip home.

There was no reason during those drab weeks to ponder geology, about which they knew little, and most of all vulcanology. The only book Jefferson had on the subject, Claude Nicholas Ordinare's *Histoire naturelle des volcans* (Paris, 1802), he did not purchase until the expedition was on its way. And Ordinare could have known nothing of the great "ring of fire" around the Pacific Basin, bubbling with underground lava which occasionally burst forth from one of the rumbling cones. A prominent feature of this ring was the Cascade Range. The snow-clad volcanic peaks of that range were not extinct; they were only sleeping, and some merely napping.

All these peaks had erupted periodically since ancient times. Vancouver appeared to know nothing of these events, but Spanish schooners in 1792, checking out the Bellingham Bay area, reported thunderings and fiery flashes to the east that probably were signs that Mount Baker (north of Mount Rainier) was erupting. Mount St. Helens, the most restless one, would be active in later years, with a great eruption occurring in 1842 and a spectacular and devastating one in 1980. The periods between these perturbations, considered geologically, were of course tiny indeed.

Lewis and Clark began their homeward journey in the spring of 1806. On their way back up the Columbia, they discovered a peak lying to the southeast that somehow they had missed on the way down the river. "This is a noble mountain," Clark wrote, "and I think equally as high or something higher than Mt. St. Heleans . . . its figure is a regular cone and is covered with eternial snow."

They named it Mount Jefferson. They could not know that it had erupted about 950 B.C., and undoubtedly still seethed with glowing fires beneath its quiet snow. The man for whom it was named, and who had instructed Lewis and Clark to look for evidence of volcanoes, was never to realize that his team of explorers had found such evidence in abundance, and that the memorial they had created for him was one of the slumbering, smoldering giants of the Pacific ring of fire.

Home to the Unknown

*T*he exuberant members of the expedition were forming up for the final descent of the Missouri. During the homeward journey they had been divided into groups from time to time, performing chores they had devised for themselves during the rainy winter at Fort Clatsop. They were still traveling in two groups, Lewis leading one and Clark the other, but were only a day apart. Tomorrow they would be united again. It was 11 August 1806.

They were accustomed to shortages by now — food, tobacco, whiskey — but soon these wants would be satisfied. The deprivation they seemed to feel most keenly was the lack of news. Was there war or peace? Which fathers or mothers had died without a last goodbye to their sons? What crops had failed, what mill dams washed away, what farms foreclosed upon?

To the captains, not knowing how one particular man was faring must have been excruciating. They did not even know if Thomas Jefferson was still president of the United States.

Jefferson was nearing the end of his first term when the expedition had pushed away from the river shore and turned westward in May 1804. Lewis and Clark had passed the first winter with the Mandans, most of their effort going into the collecting of data, the drawing of maps, the packing of natural history specimens for the President who had conceived, sponsored, and helped to plan their undertaking. During that time, Jefferson had won enough electoral votes to assure him of a second term by a victory over Charles C. Pinckney, and he was inaugurated in March 1805. A month later, Lewis and Clark had dispatched a keelboat to St. Louis, partly to return men no longer needed but most particularly to send their accumulated information and specimens to Jefferson. Then, not sure if he was still their president, they had proceeded on toward the Pacific.

The first to encounter white men on the return trip was Clark, who had come rapidly down the Yellowstone and entered the Missouri, leaving a note for Lewis at the confluence of the rivers. On 11 August, at

Little Knife Creek, he and his men were astonished to encounter two American trappers who were much farther up the Missouri than Clark would have expected, and probably were the only whites to have come this far since Lewis and Clark had themselves passed up the river a year and a half ago.

Hungry as Clark and his band were for news from home, they were to meet disappointment upon questioning the pair. Joseph Dixon and Forrest Hancock, from the St. Louis area, had been on the river since the late summer of 1804 and were thus ignorant of recent happenings back in the United States. Dixon might otherwise have been a useful informant, as he was a literate man who was later to serve as an election judge and strong supporter of a school system in Sangamon County, Illinois. No news of Jefferson or of political affairs came from this source, but nevertheless Dixon and Hancock were soon to play an interesting role in the history of the expedition.

Clark traveled on, and Lewis's detachment met Dixon and Hancock the next day. Lewis was painfully disabled, having been shot accidentally in the left thigh by one of his men. He conferred with the two trappers, gave them some powder and lead, and learned from them that Clark was not far downstream. Apparently the accounts given the trappers by Lewis and Clark were enough to persuade them that they might find themselves outmanned by Indians, so they decided to follow the expedition back down to the Hidatsa and Mandan villages to recruit a partner, perhaps a Frenchman.

At the villages—where Lewis and Clark were greeted with enthusiasm by Indian friends they had made two winters earlier—one of their best men decided he wanted to join trappers Dixon and Hancock and return to the mountains. He was John Colter, now better known in the legends of the West for his exploits in the upper Yellowstone country than for his contributions to the Lewis and Clark story. Living up to our image of the mountain man in western American history, he seemed perfectly willing to forego a visit with family and friends after long months of travel, and to hop into a boat going back into the wilderness.

The question of whether Jefferson was still in office bore some relevance to the actions of Lewis and Clark at the Indian villages. They sent out word that important men of the tribes were invited to descend the river and visit their Great Father in Washington. This was an aspect of their expedition to which Jefferson had attached real importance, but a new president might not be so interested. Still, these invitations were a part of their instructions, and Lewis and Clark tried hard to find chiefs willing to make the journey. Only Sheheke, of the Mandans, volunteered to go with his wife, son, and a halfblood interpreter.

Lewis's wound was serious enough so that he lay helpless in the boat as the expedition moved downstream. As Clark wrote in his journal, "Capt. Lewis's wounds are heeling very fast. I am much in hope of his being able to walk in 8 or 10 days."

They met three Frenchmen on the morning of 21 August, including two men who had wintered with them at the Mandans, plus a young boy who was anxious to return home. Lewis and Clark gave him passage. From these men they learned that an Arikara chief who had accepted their invitation to go east, in the summer of 1804, had died on the journey. As the Arikaras were occasionally hostile anyway, this event could have been an unhappy omen for the prospects of peace on the river.

Lewis walked a bit on the 22nd. Clark removed the gauze packing that had been keeping his wound open so that it could drain properly and heal from the bottom. Another ten days were to ensue before they were to encounter another white man; he was James Aird, an intelligent, active trader on both the Missouri and the Mississippi rivers, whose permanent headquarters was at Prairie du Chien on the Upper Mississippi. Here at last was someone the explorers could pump for news of home. "Our first enquirey," Clark wrote, "was after the President of our country and then our friends and the State of the politics of our country &c." This is strong evidence that Lewis and Clark had not been sure until now how Jefferson had fared in the last election. Clark sat up late with Aird, taking shelter in his tent during a rainstorm, and talked of home. "This Gentleman informed us of maney changes," Clark reported. General James Wilkinson, commanding general of the U.S. army with headquarters at St. Louis, had been ordered south to the Sabine to deal with a boundary dispute with the Spaniards. Aird told of a war with Tripoli which had begun and ended while the expedition had been in progress. He said that two British warships had fired on an American ship in the port of New York. He told of two Indians being hanged in St. Louis for murder. And there was the shocking story of a duel fought between Aaron Burr and Alexander Hamilton, in which Hamilton had been killed.

The encounter in New York harbor was an outgrowth of British incursions on American neutrality in the war between Great Britain and France. British vessels had been impounding American cargo, impressing American seamen, and generally behaving in a way that would eventually lead to the embargo of 1807. Off Sandy Hook, H.M.S. *Leander* had fired a shot intended to force an American vessel to heave to for a search.

The cannonball had killed a man on another American vessel. As a result, Jefferson had issued a proclamation charging the captain with murder and ordering three British vessels out of American waters.

The Burr-Hamilton duel must have distressed Lewis, who had come to know both men intimately during his service as the President's aide and secretary. Burr had been Jefferson's vice-president and Hamilton a former Federalist cabinet member while Lewis was on Jefferson's staff. Aird's account must have been both sketchy and tantalizing.

"Our party appears extreamly anxious to get on," Clark wrote. Lewis was almost completely healed, able to "walk and even run nearly as well as ever he could."

Encounters with Americans from St. Louis were becoming more frequent. As always, the captains and their men were hungry for news and added bits and pieces with every encounter. Always pointing out that he acted "for the men," Clark bartered for whiskey when he could. One trader charged him eight dollars for a two-gallon cask, which Clark considered outrageous.

A Frenchman identified by Clark as "Alexander La fass" passed the expedition on the way to the Pawnees. He reported that Lieutenant Zebulon Pike, accompanied by General Wilkinson's son James, had left St. Louis on a reconnaissance to the West in the general direction of Santa Fe. Pike, who had known Lewis when they were both paymasters for their regiments, was to become lost while searching for the headwaters of the Red River and fall temporarily into the hands of the Spaniards in Mexico.

The expedition stopped at the grave of Sergeant Charles Floyd, who had died on the upriver trip, and repaired the site. Clark noticed a number of young black walnut trees near the grave, one more sign of a changing flora.

A meeting with Joseph Gravelines, a government interpreter for the Arikaras, provided another reminder that Thomas Jefferson was still a presence in the lives of the Indians. Gravelines was carrying a speech written by Jefferson to be read to the Arikaras, consoling them for the loss of a favorite chief who had died during a trip to Washington. "Man must die, at home or abroad," Jefferson had said in one of the several letters of consolation he wrote as a consequence of such visitations. The chiefs were low in immunity to the white man's diseases and to the stresses of such trips.

Two men with similar names, often confused in history, appeared next. The first was Robert McClellan, a well-known trader. He was an old army acquaintance from the days when both Lewis and Clark had served under General Anthony Wayne on the Indian frontier of the 1790s.

Captain John McClallan appeared on 17 September, a recently retired army officer known to Lewis and Clark as a close associate of General Wilkinson. He was taking trade goods for the Omahas and said he might make an excursion in the direction of Santa Fe. As he was never to be heard from again, and as anyone connected with General Wilkinson was suspected of opportunism, exactly what McClallan was doing has always been a mystery.

That Lewis and Clark would need to get used to changes in St. Louis officialdom was inevitable. On a trading license issued to Joseph Robidoux, they puzzled over the name of Joseph Browne—the acting governor of Upper Louisiana in the absence of General Wilkinson.

Although they had bartered for a barrel of flour and other foodstuffs, they were running low. The captains rationed the flour, but by 18 September the men were subsisting mainly on papaws picked from trees along the shore. Never mind, they told their commanders; they could live on a few papaws and great expectations for the rest of the trip.

One of the famous phrases in the journals of the expedition had been written when Pacific waters had come into view. "Ocian in view! O the joy," Clark had written. Now he penned another heartfelt expression of pleasure at a more prosaic discovery: "We saw some cows on the bank which was a joyfull Sight to the party and caused a Shout to be raised for joy."

The next day they reached St. Charles and could feel that they were all but home, for that little village not far from St. Louis contained friends, good food, and fellowship. Arriving on Sunday, they stayed two days, enjoying French hospitality and writing letters that could be rushed overland to the postmaster at Cahokia, across the Mississippi from St. Louis. In Clark's words, "We saluted the Village by three rounds from our blunderbuts and the Small arms of the party, and landed near the lower part of the town. We were met by great numbers of the inhabitants, we found them excessively polite. . . . The inhabitants of this village appear much delighted at our return and seem to vie with each other in their politeness to us all." The rewards for long months of hardship and sheer suffering were beginning, and the expedition had not even reached their real destination of St. Louis.

Something had happened during the descent of the Missouri that could not have escaped the attention of the captains. They had met about a hundred and fifty men from the settled areas, going up the river in keelboats and pirogues laden with trade goods. Most of these were nameless French *voyageurs,* but many were entrepreneurs who were now about to capitalize on the good will, the information, and the precedents set by Lewis and Clark. A new post-expedition era had begun; the captains were coming back to a world that was changed, and they had done much to change it.

William Clark and the Girls on the Pony

$\mathbf{S}$itting on the bank of a Montana stream, William Clark mused, "I know but one other spot so beautiful. I will name this river for my little mountain maid of Fincastle, the Judith." It did not happen that way, and the incident as imagined by a popular writer illustrates a problem that historians frequently have in dealing with family tradition.

At the beginning of the twentieth century, a novelist and devotee of western American history published *The Conquest* (Chicago, 1902). Although this work by Eva Emery Dye was primarily about the Lewis and Clark Expedition, the author's broad interests led her to include sections on the American Revolution in the Ohio Valley, the Black Hawk War, the role of Tecumseh in the War of 1812, Clark's later career, and the great emigration movement to Oregon in the 1840s.

Mrs. Dye had published verse in Illinois newspapers under the name of Jenny Juniper during her teens. After marrying a classmate at Oberlin College, she moved to Oregon City, Oregon, to spend her life writing novels and local history. In collecting data for *The Conquest,* she did the usual library research and corresponded with such descendants of Lewis and Clark as the grandsons of Clark, the widows of Clark's sons, an heir of Lewis's, and "more than twenty nieces and nephews." Although the original journals of the expedition had not yet been published, Mrs. Dye gained access to them through editor Reuben Gold Thwaites. She also used the letterbooks that Clark had kept during his long tenure as superintendent of Indian affairs with headquarters in St. Louis.

She thus had the basic facts at her disposal for a factual portrayal of the expedition and its members. But she chose to relate "The True Story of Lewis and Clark," as the subtitle reads, while composing it in the form of a novel. Historical novelists often appear to want it both ways. They can cram a manuscript with fact, but when gaps appear in the factual record, the easy option lies in the use of the writer's imagination. Although the Dye novel is today widely recognized as a deceptive mixture of truth and fantasy, it is cited in the footnotes and bibliographies of a surprising number of modern historical studies.

"Through the frowning portals of Cumberland Gap, Captain Clark and his man York galloped into Virginia. . . . Cantering thoughtfully along under the broad-leaved locusts and laurels, a melody like the laugh of wood-nymphs ripped from the forest."

" 'Why don't he go?' cried a musical feminine voice. 'Oh, Harriet, Harriet!' With more laughter came a rustling of green leaves. Parting the forest curtain to discover the source of this unusual commotion, Captain Clark descried two girls seated on a small pony, switching with all their slender energy."

In this way, says Mrs. Dye, Clark met Julia Hancock and Harriet Kennerly, two first cousins just into their teens. The fact that Clark was destined to marry Julia, and still later Harriet, was more than a novelist could resist.

"Judy's hair was a fluff of gold then; shading to brown, it was a fluff of gold still. . . . Harriet, her cousin, of dark and splendid beauty, a year or two older, was ever the inseparable companion of Judy Hancock. . . . Several times in the course of the next few years, William Clark had occasion to visit Virginia on behalf of his brother [George Rogers Clark], and each time more and more he noted the budding graces of the maids of Fincastle."

Briefly, according to the Dye account that has been borrowed in scores of retellings, the thirty-three-year-old Clark went off to explore the West with the image of a prospective child-bride in his thoughts. He named a river for her, and when he returned to the acclaim of a grateful nation, he hastened to Fincastle to woo Miss Hancock, now a beautiful lass who was by then just barely of marriageable age.

It is true that both Lewis and Clark named rivers in honor of young women they knew at home. Lewis christened the Marias for his cousin, Maria Wood. Clark named two, but his first choice was not in honor of Julia Hancock. A few miles beyond the mouth of the Yellowstone, in what is now eastern Montana, he gave the name of a river to a mysterious young woman whom he called "the selebrated M.F." Elsewhere, in a letter to his sister, he had once referred to her as the "cruel" M.F. The decision to commemorate her in Montana's topography was not an instant one; Clark's label for the river appears to have been added some time after the explorers had passed it, but before they returned to St. Louis. He called it Marthy's River. If he hoped to gain some favor with Marthy, and if indeed she was "cruel" to him, we may find some devilish satisfaction in knowing that early settlers would soon be calling the stream the Big Muddy. Never toy with the affections of our heroes, O cruel Miss F.

The idea of naming a river for Miss Hancock came much later than we have always supposed. The stream Clark chose to bear her name was first called the Big Horn on his field maps. Not even on the large, official map that he drew up for the War Department in 1806, after the expedition, did he place the name Judiths River. That name first appears on a large manuscript map that Clark kept for himself, in the early years after his return from the Pacific. A safe supposition is that he named Judiths River some time between his return from the Pacific in 1806 and his submission of the map in December 1810 to be engraved for publication.

It has been said, by writers who assume he named the river when he first encountered it, that Clark did not yet know the girl's "correct" name was Julia. But was it? When the marriage bond was posted in Botetourt County, Virginia, she was listed as Judith Hancock. She was also entered as Judith on the marriage register. In adult life she was generally to be known as Julia, even in documents relating to her estate, but there is little doubt that she began life as Judith.

As so often happens, the facts of Lewis and Clark history are gripping, poignant, and do not need embellishments provided by a novelist. Clark did court Julia, but not as a child; he did name a river for her, but only as an afterthought. And he did take her to St. Louis as his bride, but apparently not without some persuasion. After a visit to Fincastle in the spring of 1807, Clark wrote to Lewis in the kind of convoluted language that often taxes the reader of his letters and journals: "I have made an attacked most vigorously, we have come to terms, and a delivery is to be made first of January . . . when I shall be in possession highly pleasing to my self." Lewis could translate his friend's prose well enough: Clark was engaged to Julia.

Late in the winter of 1807, the two explorers were appointed to important positions in the new Louisiana Territory. Lewis became governor and Clark was made superintendent of Indian affairs and also brigadier-general of the territorial militia. Also, Lewis had negotiated a publishing contract for the journals that he and Clark had toiled over for so long, and was about to begin the laborious job of revising them.

Clark went to St. Louis to get his various assignments squared away, and returned to Virginia in the fall to make plans for his marriage. The two were wed in January 1808, in the home of Julia's father, George, an old Revolutionary War soldier, congressman, and well-known citizen of southwestern Virginia.

The arrival of the popular Clark and his sixteen-year-old bride in St. Louis was an exciting public event, appropriately imagined by Eva Emery

Dye. Lacking a contemporary account, she painted a word picture so convincing that Clark's nephew, William Clark Kennerly, who had not been present at the arrival, used her version when dictating his own memoirs about the Clark family more than ninety years later. His *Persimmon Hill* (Norman, 1948) quotes heavily from Mrs. Dye's narrative. This is how she saw the trip by boat down the Ohio and up the Mississippi:

> To Clark no spring had ever seemed so beautiful. Sitting on deck with Julia he could not forget that turbulent time when as a boy he first plunged down these waters. . . . The rough old life of camps and forts was gone forever.
>
> And to Julia, everything was new and strange, —La Belle Rivière itself whispered of Louisiana. Like an Alpine horn the bugle echoed the dreamlife of the waters.
>
> The fiddles scraping, boatmen dancing, the smooth stream rolling calmly through the forest, the girls who gathered on shore to see the pageant pass, the river itself, momentarily lost to view, then leaping again in Hogarth's line of beaty, —all murmured perpetual music. . . .
>
> One day the boats stopped, and before her Julia beheld the Mississippi sweeping with irresistible pomp and wrath, tearing at the shores, bearing upon its tawny bosom the huge drift of mount and meadow, whole herds of drowned buffalo, trunks of forest trees and caved-in banks of silt, leaping, sweeping seaward in the sun. Without a pause the bridegroom river reached forth his brawny arm, and gathered in the starry-eyed Ohio. Over his Herculean shoulders waved her silver tresses, deep into his bosom passed her gentle transparency as the twain made one swept to the honeymoon. . . .
>
> On the 26th of May Governor Lewis received a letter from Clark asking for help up the river. Without delay the Governor engaged a barge to take their things to Bellefontaine and another barge to accommodate the General, his family and baggage.
>
> Dispatching a courier over the Bellefontaine road, Governor Lewis sent to Colonel Hunt a message, asking him to send Ensign Pryor to meet the party.
>
> With what delight Clark and his bride saw the barges with Ensign Pryor in charge, coming down from St. Louis. Then came the struggle up the turbulent river. Clark was used to such things, but never before had he looked on them with a bride at his side. With sails and oars and cordelles all at once, skilled hands paddled and poled and stemmed the torrent, up, up to the rock of the new levee.
>
> Thus the great explorer brought home his bride to St. Louis in that never-to-be-forgotten May-time one hundred years ago.

The Clarks rented a house at Pine and Main streets, and Lewis is said to have occupied rooms there so the two men could work on their journals. The house became a gathering place for the socially well-endowed of St. Louis, especially after Julia's piano was uncrated and her musical talent became known.

Within a year the Clarks were planning a trip back East, William traveling on business and Julia no doubt eager to see her family. Government employees in the West always seemed to arrange their eastern trips so that winter would close in and keep them off the job for a longer stay. The Clarks arranged to set out in September by land, knowing it would be impossible for them to return over crude roads or on frozen rivers until spring.

At the same time, Lewis also was heading for Washington by a different route. Both men had received some criticism from their superiors, but Lewis's problems were the most severe, involving disallowed expenditures for which he was being held personally responsible. By now, Lewis was laboring under an insuperable burden of alcoholism that was of great concern to Clark and a public scandal in St. Louis.

The entourage that crossed the Mississippi 21 September 1809 included a carriage with extra riding horses, two black servants named Chloe and Scot, and an eight-month-old baby son, Meriwether Lewis Clark. Their route was to take them south to Kaskaskia, the capital of the newly formed Illinois Territory, then east through swampy country to Shawneetown, and to the ferry across the Ohio. The accommodations were so unpleasant that at one tavern or ordinary, where they stopped to spend the night but found no food ready, Julia and Chloe killed two chickens for dinner.

At Russellville, Kentucky, they stayed with the Temple family and Julia found a tempting recipe for pickles. She copied it for future use:

Mrs. Temples receipt for making green Sweet Meats

Let your cucumbers or muskmellons (or such fruit as you wish) lay in salt water untill they turn yellow, then boil them in spring water until they cook plump. If they will not green as deep as you want them throw a small bit of allum in while boiling. Have your cirrup ready to lay them in before they get cold or else they will all draw up. The ginger must be soaked well before it is put in.

They spent two weeks in Louisville, visiting with William's brother, the famed George Rogers Clark, and other members of the large Clark family, then left for Virginia on 26 October. Between Louisville and Lexington a copy of the Frankfort *Argus* fell into Clark's hands, and he read the shattering news that was soon to sweep the nation and throw his own life into turmoil. Meriwether Lewis was dead, killed by gunshot wounds at a tavern on the Natchez Trace. "I fear, O! I fear the weight of his mind has overcome him," Clark exclaimed in a letter to his brother Jonathan. "What will be the Consequence? What will become of his papers?" His assumption that the death was a suicide would eventually become the accepted one, although the possibility of murder would also be widely discussed.

Assuming responsibility for the recovery and publication of the Lewis and Clark journals, Clark hurried on to the Wilderness Road, through the Cumberland Gap, and into Virginia. He left Julia and the baby at Fincastle, proceeding to Charlottesville and Monticello, where he first visited Lewis's mother and then Thomas Jefferson.

Julia sent with him a list of things to do. She wanted some silks dyed, and ordered "one fashionable dress any thing but thin Muslin." And she asked him to obtain a "necklace and braselets of linked hair. If you would have J H C put in gold letters in the clasps it would be much handsomer."

In Washington, Clark conferred with William Eustis, the secretary of war, and did what he could to bring some order into Lewis's official affairs. In Philadelphia he met with his publisher, and tried to find somebody to assist him with the preparation of the journals. He was told by publisher John Conrad that Lewis had submitted not a page of manuscript in the thirty months since signing a contract. Only after Clark had returned to Fincastle did he learn of the willingness of Nicholas Biddle, an active and enthusiastic litterateur, to write a narrative based on the journals. Biddle traveled to Fincastle in April to consult with Clark and take extensive notes, and then the Clarks continued on to St. Louis.

Uppermost in the minds of all who lived in the Mississippi Valley was the growing tension between the United States and England, and the attempt of British traders and other agents to recruit the many Indian tribes to their cause. The matter was of official concern to Clark in his roles as Indian agent and ranking officer of the militia, and the safety of his family was a personal concern.

Forts had sprung up on the Missouri and Mississippi. Clark had traveled in the fall of 1808 to a high bluff on the Missouri, about 340 miles west of St. Louis, to supervise the building of Fort Osage. At the same time, a company from the First Infantry had moved north, to a spot on the Mississippi just above the mouth of the Des Moines, and had built Fort Madison. These two posts, along with the older Fort Belle Fontaine, on the Missouri not far from St. Louis, were intended partly to protect the government factories or trading houses that did business with the Indians, and partly to control the tribes that were often hostile toward each other, but more generally hostile to the Americans.

A warlike band of Sauks and Foxes, whose homeland lay mostly in the territory of Illinois, fought openly on the British side in actions that occurred in the Ohio Valley. Their war chief, Black Hawk, and his followers made annual trips to Fort Malden, a British post in Canada, to receive presents, supplies, and beguiling promises. Indian-American relations faltered badly after the Battle of Tippecanoe, in Indiana, in November 1811.

Clark took his wife and young family out of the danger area in the spring of the following year, a move that may have been unseemly for the commander of militia in the eyes of less mobile residents of St. Louis. In a letter to Nicholas Biddle, written from Washington in August 1812, Clark said that Mrs. Clark and his two young sons would remain at Fincastle "untill our deficultes are adjusted to the N.W."

Problems arising from the financial situation of his publisher were Clark's reason for asking the Secretary of War if he could spend the winter in the East. He appears to have received permission and to have taken Julia to Philadelphia for medical treatment. By the autumn of 1814 the family had returned to St. Louis, but Clark was again planning a trip to Philadelphia, where Julia would consult a famous physician, Dr. Philip Syng Physick.

For the next several years, Julia's health was her family's biggest worry. She was confined to her bed in the spring of 1816 with a disease that was to be diagnosed as cancer. Clark became governor of Missouri Territory in 1813, while retaining his post as superintendent of Indian affairs. The times were turbulent, and in a letter to Jefferson he seemed defensive about his handling of these positions. "I am happy to have it in my power to say to you that I suceed in Keeping the Indians of the Territory (except those high up the Mississippi) in peace." But of his role in political life he complained: "Laterly a small and disappointed party has spring up determined to vex & teaze the executive."

His life with Julia was the most vigorous period in his civilian career. The glow of fame still shone brightly, and Clark's two positions made him one of the most important figures in the territory. Fur traders clamored for his favors in licensing, and men seeking wealth and position in other fields needed his friendship and cooperation. He dabbled in the fur trade himself, undisturbed by a seeming conflict of interest. He was educating two of Sacagawea's children and keeping in touch with other members of the expedition. For Julia he built a handsome brick house on Main Street, with a wing for his own offices and a large council chamber, filled with Indian artifacts but doubling as a ballroom when Julia so decreed.

When Julia's health seemed precarious in 1819, her St. Louis physician prescribed a sea voyage (by way of New Orleans) and some time in the mountains of Virginia. She was taken to the warm springs to try the healing waters, but did not improve and had to be returned to Fincastle in a bed. While her family treated her with tar fumes, Clark reluctantly left her and went St. Louis.

He had made still another trip to her bedside, and back to his duties, when he received word of Julia's death in June 1820. Once more he returned to Fincastle, where his wife was buried on a mountainside. After daughter Mary died a few months later, the surviving family included four sons—Meriwether Lewis Clark, William Preston Clark, George Rogers Hancock Clark, and Julius Clark.

The little girl whom Clark first saw on a pony—if family legend is true—had spent a brief and often sickly life on the burgeoning frontier. And now the other girl on the pony, slightly older and already a widow with three children, took Julia's place.

Harriet Kennerly Radford married Clark a year after Julia's death, and was to bear him two more sons. Having no river of her own, Harriet has not played a large role in Lewis and Clark lore. She was a busy and popular St. Louis hostess, and the life of the Clarks was solid and respectable. William was fifty-one at the time of their marriage. Dining with him and John C. Calhoun a few years later, a diarist found him "hale, of florid complexion, flaxen hair, stout pleasant countenance." The decade of the 1820s brought statehood to Missouri, relieving Clark of the territorial governorship. An unstoppable lobby consisting of Thomas Hart Benton, John Jacob Astor, and other proponents of Manifest Destiny put the federal government out of the Indian trade, diminishing Clark's influence and narrowing his duties.

Clark feared that the Indians in his charge were losing their old way of life. To Jefferson, an old man in 1826, he wrote: "In my present Situation of Superentendent of Indian Affairs, it would afford me pleasure to be enabled to meliorate the condition of those unfortunate people placed under my charge, knowing as I do their wretchedness, and their rapid decline. It is to be lamented that this deplorable Situation of the Indians do not Receive more of the humain feelings of this Nation."

During this period Clark scrawled on the cover of a notebook a roster of the persons who had gone with him to the Pacific, and indicated what had happened to them. More than half were dead. Clark included Sacagawea among the deceased, settling the question—when the notebook was discovered more than a century later—of when the Indian woman had died (she had not lived to be an old woman on a Wyoming reservation, as many had thought).

The image of Clark the explorer was diminishing. The public had little access to the record of the expedition, although the hordes who streamed westward were part of a great movement that Lewis and Clark had made possible. Even the route had changed. The wagon trains straining toward Oregon and California went up the Platte and North Platte and across South Pass in the Rockies, which was unknown when Lewis and Clark had followed a more northerly course.

Harriet died in 1831, having been a mother equally devoted to Julia's children and her own. She had given William Clark another decade of strength with which to arbitrate, temporize, and fend off the inevitable decline of the tribes. Clark had placed himself between the flood of westward immigrants and his Indian wards, and for a while stemmed the tide. He could scarcely have done more.

After Harriet's death William's powers seemed to wane. His participation in the Black Hawk War of of 1832, caused by the attempt of the "British band" to return to their Illinois lands, appears to have been equivocal, as if he could not support the Indians in a course of action against which he had advised, but also could not go wholeheartedly to war against them.

The slaughter of the errant Sauk families on the Upper Mississippi was an indecency that Clark could not have prevented but might have protested. He was entitled to even greater outrage, however, by a failure of his government that brought on the extermination of the Mandans by smallpox. Again, in this case, he appeared not so much uncertain as uninformed.

In 1832 the U.S. government had decided to fight a severe outbreak of a disease that periodically raged through both white and red populations. Congress provided funds, and stipulated it to be the duty of Indian agents under the Secretary of War to put a smallpox vaccination program into effect. Two doctors were hired to treat the Indians on the Missouri, including such northern tribes as the Arikaras and Mandans. Their work went well during the first season, but they were unable to complete their assignment before winter overtook them. They reported to Secretary of War Lewis Cass that they needed permission to return the next spring, to finish their work among the Arikaras and to vaccinate the Mandans.

Secretary Cass appears to have decided on his own, despite his instructions from Congress, not to extend the project into the second year. Worse, he led Congress to believe that the task was being finished. The debacle that followed, after half the Arikaras and all the Mandans were left untreated, seems almost surely to have been the fault of Cass alone.

In the spring of 1837 smallpox broke out on the Upper Missouri, then raged among the Arikaras and the Mandans. The epidemic took lives in most of the tribes along the Missouri, but was far less severe among tribes that had been vaccinated. By February 1838, Clark was reporting to his superiors that the Mandan nation had been reduced to a handful of persons.

It is difficult to tell from his papers whether Clark felt partly responsible for the genocidal neglect of the tribe that, more than any other, had befriended him and his colleagues during the expedition to the Pacific. In his last years he had deferred to his chief clerk in handling matters of this kind, and he seemed undisturbed when Cass, and Indian commissioner Elbert Herring in the Department of War, ignored his role as ombudsman for the western tribes. Hindsight must be used with care here, so that the reputation of one of the last Jeffersonians on the frontier is not carelessly tarnished. Clark was a fragile old man when his longtime friends, the Mandans, suffered the apocalyptic scourge of 1837. An entire people died, and he seemed not to understand what had caused the holocaust.

Clark's own losses in a lifetime on the frontier had been substantial. He had lost his best friend Meriwether Lewis to the ravages of alcohol (and in 1838, the year of his death, one of his own sons was himself fighting alcoholism). He had lost Sacagawea, Colter, Floyd, Drouillard, Pryor, and many others on that roll call of gallant explorers. He had lost one at a time the maidens on their stubborn little horse, from the blue hills of Virginia. He had lost the Mandans, all of them, by an unbelievable error of another man's judgment.

But his memories, as he lay dying, must have been glorious.

A Dog Named Scannon — Until Recently

We could call this simply the tale of a man and his dog, roaming the High Plains and the passes of the Rockies in one of our great sagas of western exploration. For me, however, it gets better when I see it also as proof that there is still fun to be had in the writing of American history.

It supports a maxim that I have learned in reading the scrawls of our forebears, found in the diaries, letters, and state papers that have been the basis of historical research since written records began: the two ways to decipher an unreadable word or passage in a handwritten document are either to stare at it thoughtfully — for a very long time, if necessary — or on rare occasions to experience a soul-satisfying flash of sudden recognition.

Lewis and Clark enthusiasts had to wait for a century to learn that Lewis had a dog. Nicholas Biddle failed to mention the animal at all in his narrative of the expedition. When Reuben Gold Thwaites edited and published the journals of the explorers, in 1904-5, he made no comment on the various references to "our dog" or "Capt. Lewis's dog," although he listed several allusions to him under "dogs" in the index of his edition.

Sergeant John Ordway, whose journal of the expedition was not published until 1916, wrote on 18 April 1805, "One man killed another goose and Scannon brought him out." Here at last was a dog with a name, a creature who hunted birds, pulled pronghorns out of the river, scampered with the men, and worried his master by staying away from camp all night.

Lewis identified his dog as being "of the newfoundland breed," and thus gave him an origin and a persona. Newfoundlands are handsome black dogs that seem to bear some of the characteristics of the people among whom they evolved: "Scannon's ancestors originated in the north-eastern corner of Spain, where the Pyrenees Mountains come down to the sea. Here live the Basques . . . a fiercely independent, freedom-loving people who have for centuries fought the power of their Spanish masters," Ernest S. Osgood wrote in a sketch of "Scannon." They herded sheep intelligently and tirelessly among the Basques, and took readily to the water when their masters became fisherman off the Grand Banks of Newfoundland.

The dog probably came into Lewis's life during the final weeks of preparation for the expedition, perhaps not until the departure from Pittsburgh for the descent of the Ohio. He was to become one of the "novelty" members of the expedition, like the young Indian woman Sacagawea, or Clark's slave, York, useful to historians and artists who were interested in the social history of the undertaking. After publication of Sergeant Ordway's journal, the dog began to appear in murals and illustrations. Robert Scriver, a well-known sculptor of western subjects, produced a bronze statuette of Lewis and his dog Scannon, distributed by the Lewis and Clark Trail Heritage Foundation. Historian Ernest S. Osgood's sensitive piece about Scannon's long trek across the continent and back soon appeared on the appropriate reading lists.

I became involved in Scannon's story rather by accident when I was doing a study of Lewis and Clark place-names in Montana (published in this volume). I had learned that the explorers were direct and simple in their selection of names for streams, mountains, and other natural features. Although now and then they came up with an unworkable and ill-chosen name such as Philanthropy River, or No Preserves Island, they usually went straight to the heart of the matter and chose a sound, reasonable name to commemorate a member or sponsor of the expedition, to describe the terrain, or to recall an incident along the route.

Having become comfortable in the belief that I could nearly always discover the reason for one of their place-names, I was perplexed to find that in western Montana, during his return trip in 1806, Lewis had given the name Seaman's Creek to a northern tributary of the Blackfoot River.

No person named Seaman is known to have been associated with the lives of either captain, and as a common term the word seemed strangely out of place in Montana. Elliott Coues was puzzled by the name in his edition of the Biddle narrative: "A name I believe not found elsewhere in this History, and to the personality of which I have no clew."

The thought occurred to me that the name might be a garbled version of Scannon's Creek, to commemorate the dog. Scannon had been with Lewis on that side trip, and no geographical feature had yet been named for him during the entire expedition. But when I consulted microcopies of the journals, half suspecting I would find that Seaman's Creek was actually Scannon's Creek, what I learned instead was mildly startling: the stream was named Seaman's Creek *because the dog's name was Seaman.*

For verification I asked two members of the library staff at the American Philosophical Society in Philadelphia, holder of the original journals, to look at the occurrences of the name in the manuscript. The opinion of Murphy D. Smith and Beth Carroll-Horrocks is summed up in a letter from Mrs. Carroll-Horrocks: "It sure looks like S-e-a-m-o-n to me."

"Scannon" is one of three readings of the dog's name given by Milo M. Quaife in his edition of Ordway's journal. Quaife also transcribed the name as "Scamon" and "Semon." Ink has a way of spreading as the years pass, so that an *e* might fill in to resemble the letter *c*. An *m* can be misread as *nn* by the most careful of editors. Quaife transcribed the name as he saw it and did not speculate on which spelling might be the "correct" one.

Confronted by the name in William Clark's field notes, Ernest S. Osgood noted the variant spellings that Quaife had used, but opted for Scannon as the preferred name. When he wrote a piece for *Montana, the Magazine of Western History,* it was entitled "Our Dog Scannon—Partner in Discovery." The article later was distributed as a separate publication by the Lewis and Clark Trail Heritage Foundation, Inc. (Also see Osgood in the list of sources.)

Until this time, no one had any reason to doubt the name. When the Foundation issued its notable bronze by Scriver in 1976, the title inscribed on its base was "Meriwether Lewis and Our Dog Scannon."

Once we become alert to the existence of the correct name, it jumps at us from the manuscript and printed journals, even though both Clark and Ordway spelled it Seamon instead of Seaman. A reader might look at one occurrence of the name in the journals and read it "Scannon," but the whole of the evidence leaves no doubt that the word is Seaman.

About the origin of the name we can only speculate, bearing in mind that Lewis might have picked up the dog along the wharves of Philadelphia or Pittsburgh, and perhaps liked the way his new companion took to life in a keelboat and on the water during the descent of the Ohio River from Pittsburgh in 1803.

As Monture Creek the stream enters the Blackfoot River in Powell County, Montana, crossing under state highway 200 a few miles west of Ovando. It seems to have gone unnamed until the late nineteenth century, when it was reportedly named for George Monture, killed by Indians in the area. As a family name, Monture apparently is derived from such early Montanans as Nicholas Monteur, a trader operating on the Kootenai for the North West Company in 1811, and his son or nephew David, who served with the American Fur Company in the 1830s.

Trivial or not, the name of the expedition mascot has been of great interest to Lewis and Clark enthusiasts. Why did they have to wait 180 years to learn it? Nicholas Biddle, had he put the name into his notes when he interviewed Clark in the spring of 1810, before his preparation of the first narrative, could have handled the matter nicely. The dog was not mentioned by name until the appearance of Ordway's journal in 1916. At that time all the materials for the identification of the animal were at hand—but nobody noticed. Osgood, the first historian to take a sentimental dog-lover's interest in Seaman, was profiling a "member" of the expedition almost as a literary lark, and apparently considered the name Scannon to be sufficient for his purposes without speculation.

Perhaps only a student pondering the origin of the name "Seaman's Creek" in the journals, and already aware of the likelihood that the name had some connection with the expedition itself, could have made the connection. It might have happened decades ago, or not for another fifty years.

The illustrations that follow include most occurrences of the name Seaman in the journals. Because explanations of the figures are often too long to go under the facsimiles, they are presented here.

Figs. 1 and 2. Compare Clark's writing of "Cap. Lewis's Dog Seamon" with "To Seamons Creek." Clark spelled the name as he heard it, perhaps never having seen it in print. The first instance is from his journal entry of 5 July 1804, when the expedition was in present Atchinson County, Kansas, and it is reproduced in Osgood, Doc. 28. The second is from Clark's "Summary Statement of Rivers [and] Creeks and most remarkable places" (Thwaites, 6:72).

Fig. 3. Lewis's only writing of "Seaman's Creek," in an entry dated 5 July 1806, when he is separated from Clark and traveling in present Powell County, Montana. The complete passage reads: "East 3 M. to the entrance of a large creek 20 yds. wide Called Seaman's Creek." Note that the name of the stream was entered later by Lewis, apparently not conceived at the time of discovery.

Fig. 4. In Clark's hand, this passage is based on information obtained from Lewis when the two men were again traveling together. Not published in the Thwaites edition of the journals, this entry appears in the original manuscript, Codex N, p. 147, in the American Philosophical Society Library.

Fig. 5. Ordway's writing of "Seamon" is reproduced from the original manuscript in the American Philosophical Society Library. The passage dated 26 April 1805 reads: "Saw a flock of goats Swimming the river this morning near our camp. Capt. Lewises dog Seamon took after them [and] caught one in the river." The party was near the confluence of the Yellowstone and Missouri rivers.

Fig. 6. Near present Lewiston, Idaho, on 8 May 1805, Ordway wrote: "Several of the hunters went out and killed 4 deer one of the hunters wounded a deer only broke its leg. Capt. Lewises dog Seamon chased it and caught [and] killed it."

Fig. 7. Clark's sketch map of a portion of the route followed by Lewis in July 1806, created from information given him by Lewis. Lewis's campsite for the night of 5 July 1806 is shown at the mouth of Seaman's Creek where it joins the Blackfoot. In Codex N, American Philosophical Society Library.

Fig. 8. A segment of the Ovando, Montana, quadrangle, U.S. Geological Survey maps, showing Monture Creek (Seaman's Creek of Lewis and Clark) at its junction with the Blackfoot River.

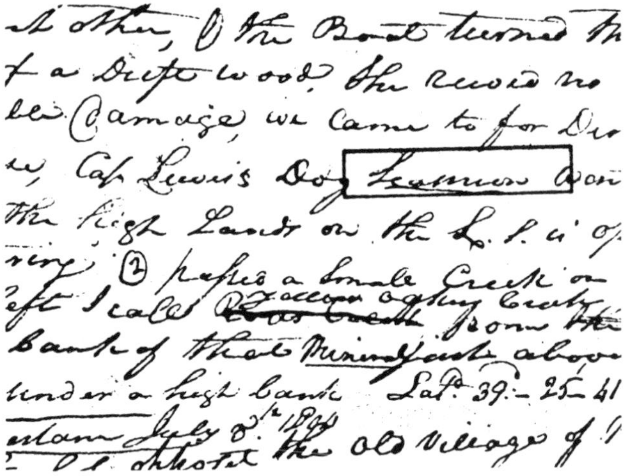

Figure 1

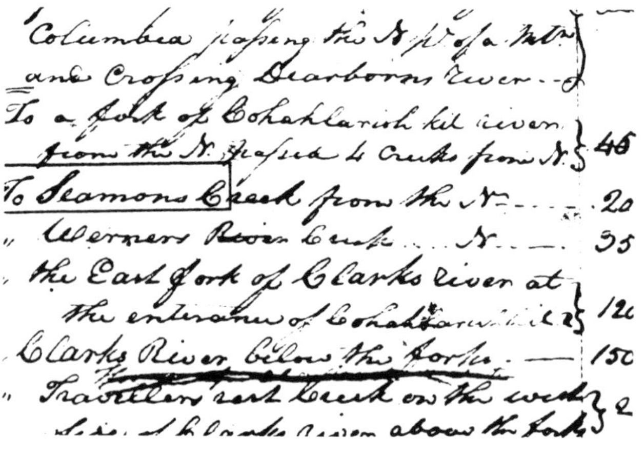

Figure 2

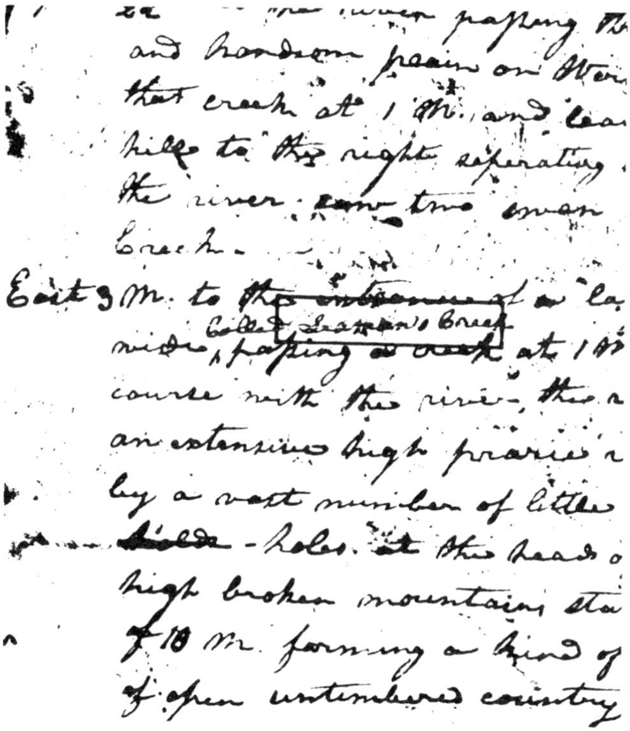
... the river passing th
and handsom plain on Win
that creek at 1 M. and lea
hills to the right seperating
the river. saw two small
Creek.
East 3 M. to the ~~entrance of a~~ la
Called Seamans Creek
wide, passing ~~a creek~~ at 1 M
course with the river, the
an extensive high prarie
by a vast number of little
~~hills~~ - holes. at the heads o
high broken mountains sta
of 10 m. forming a kind of
of open untimbered country

Figure 3

river and their course is with the u
iles to a high insulated Knob ju
entrance of a creek 3 yards wide
horges itself into Werners creek
. iles to the river passing through
plain on Werners creek crossing
ne mile and leaving a high prai
& right seperating the plain fro
er. Saw 2 Deer in this beutiful cr
els to the entrance of a large be
is wide called Leamons Creek, pass
t at 1 mile 3 yds wide (this course is
iven) the road passing through a
ew prairie, a vast number of te
s and sink holes. at the head of th
hs is high broken mountains Ela
distance of 10 m. forming a kind
naly of open untimbered country
iles to the point at which the river
etenews plains and enters the mo
plains is called the prairie of the Ti
is the North fork of Cokahlar, i

Figure 4

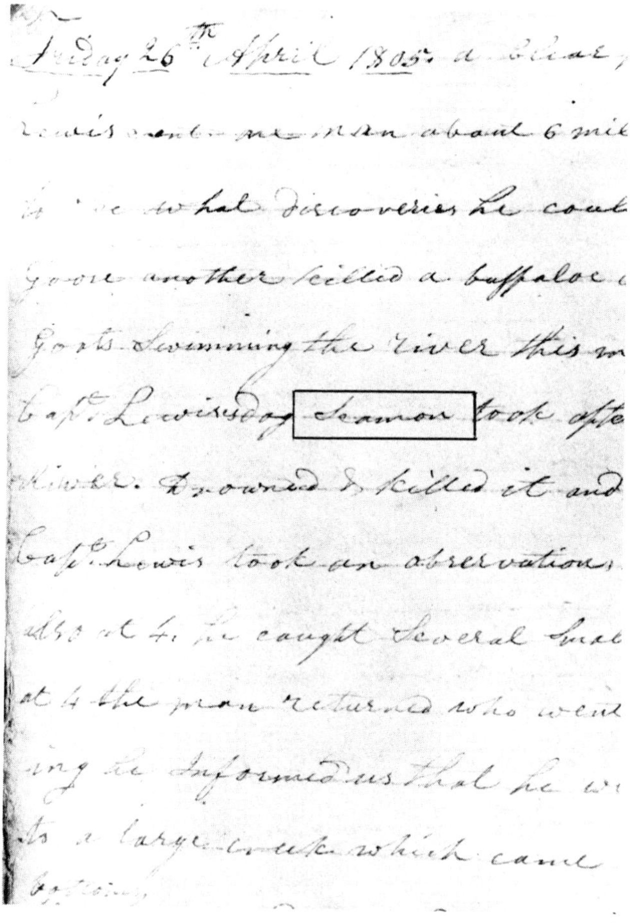
Friday 26th April 1805. a clear,
Lewis sent one man about 6 mil
see what discoveries he coul
Goose another killed a buffaloe
Goats Swimming the river this m
Capt. Lewis's dog Scamon took afte
River. Drowned & killed it and
Capt. Lewis took an observation
also at 4. he caught Several Snak
at 4 the man returned who went
ing he Informed us that he w
to a large creek which came

Figure 5

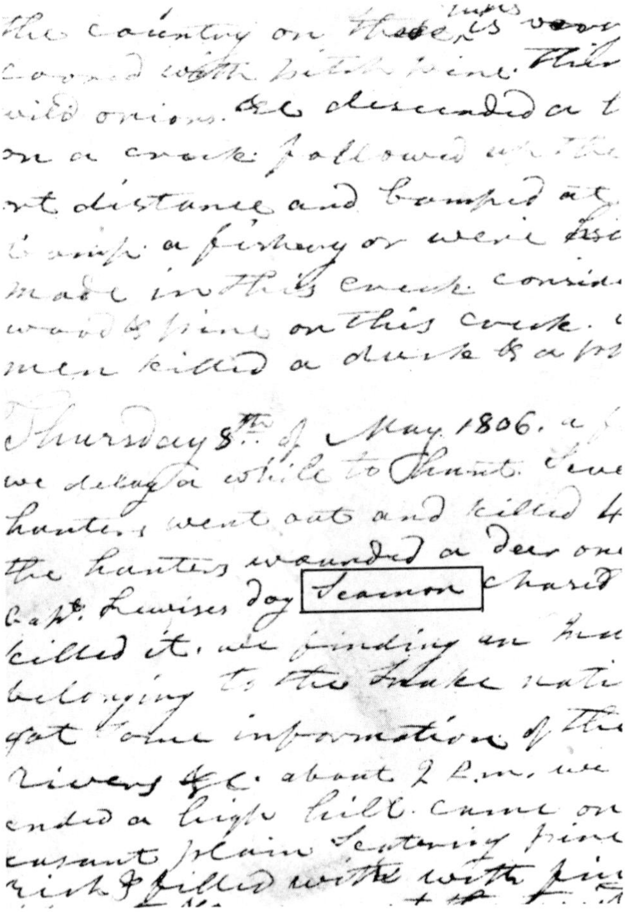
the country on those ...is verry
covered with pitch pine. there
wild onions. &c descended a ...
on a creek followed ... the
...rt distance and Camped at ...
camp. a fishery or were ...
made in this creek consid...
wood & pine on this creek. ...
men killed a duck & a ...

Thursday 8th of May 1806. a ...
we delayed a while to hunt. Seve...
hunters went out and killed 4
the hunters wounded a deer one
Capt. Lewises dog Scamon chased
killed it. we finding an Ind...
belonging to the Snake nati...
got some information of the
rivers &c. about 2 P.m. we
...ended a high hill. came on
...easant plain Scattering pine
rich & filled with with pin...

Figure 6

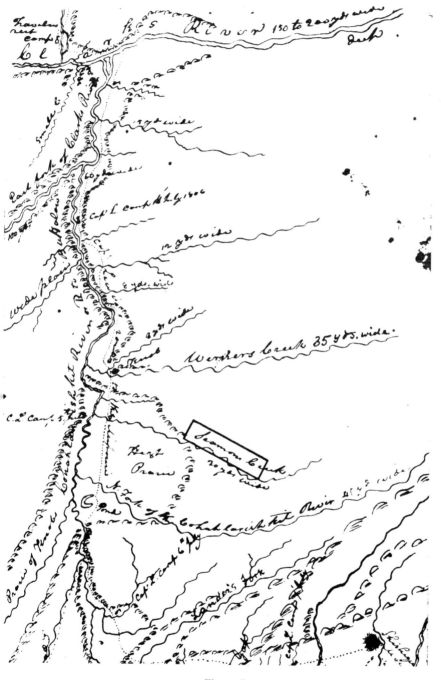

Figure 7

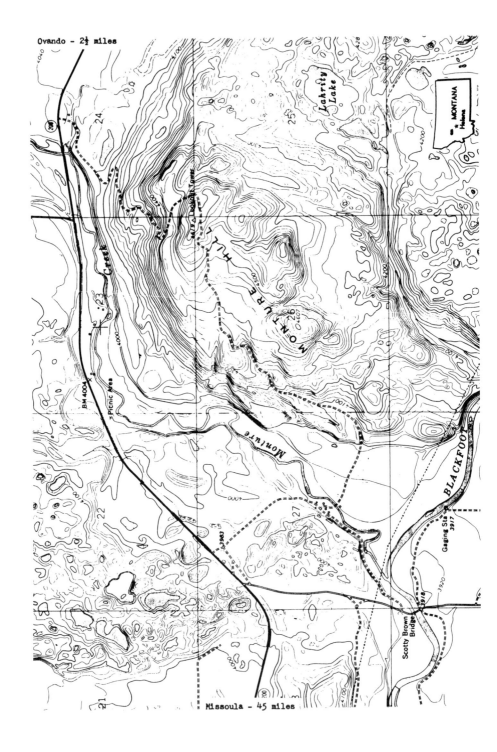

Ovando - 2¼ miles

Missoula - 45 miles

Editing the Lewis and Clark Letters

*I*n the course of a professional career I often have needed to explain to family, friends, and even to colleagues in the field of history the different meanings of the word "editor." I became editor of the University of Illinois Press in 1948, and in this role I evaluated manuscripts submitted for publication by scholars and saw their works through the publishing process. Not until several years later would I become an editor in another sense, when I began to collect, transcribe, and annotate the writings of others. What follows is an account of how I became a "documentary editor" and produced a work that has proved to be the most personally satisfying of the editions I have done.

By 1957, as an adjunct to my regular duties at the press, I had already done some historical writing and editing of my own. I had written *Custer's Gold* (New Haven, 1966), an account of Custer's 1874 expedition to the Black Hills of South Dakota, which was not to appear in print for many years because publishers were invariably disappointed to find that Custer did not die in the last chapter. I had produced a study of the War of 1812 in the middle Mississippi Valley, based on events at Fort Madison (1808–13) in what is now the state of Iowa. Unable to find a publisher, I later cannibalized the manuscript for a couple of articles, many descriptive passages, and data on the period. I even salvaged the title, *Valley Men,* for a historical novel to be published long years afterward.

The project that had led me directly into documentary editing was *Black Hawk: An Autobiography,* which I had begun to edit for publication in 1953, after I could find no scholars on my own campus or elsewhere who were prepared to do it. That study was published by Illinois in 1955, became a paperback some years later, and is still in print.

When documentary editing became a serious avocation for me, not yet a vocation, there were no guidebooks. There were no seminars such as "Camp Edit," now conducted each summer by the National Historical Publications and Records Commission. There was only the example set by editors living and dead to whose works I had been exposed: the early ones who did many things wrong but fed the fires of enthusiasm for the preservation of our documentary heritage, and the "good" new ones to whom I learned to turn for guidance, such as Clarence E. Carter and Julian P. Boyd.

Meriwether Lewis and William Clark had been on my mind for some years, for they moved through my writing as officials of the territory of Upper Louisiana after their expedition to the Pacific in 1804-6. I began to cast about for some aspect of the expedition itself, preferably a documentary one, that might occupy my attention. The basic journals and accounts of the expedition had been in print for more than half a century, primarily the Elliott Coues edition of the original 1814 narrative (New York, 1893), and the Reuben Gold Thwaites edition of the actual journals (New York, 1905-6). Bernard DeVoto had edited a concise edition of the journals (Boston, 1953) with spelling regularized and much scientific material omitted. A joint biography of the two men had been published (New York, 1947) by John Bakeless. I almost abandoned Lewis and Clark without an effort after several of my Illinois colleagues declared that the expedition had "been done."

What attracted me most were the letters generated by the expedition. Thwaites had printed about a hundred such letters and miscellaneous documents as an appendix to his edition of the journals, but he treated such material as appendectual and selected only a fraction of the manuscripts available. If I expanded a potential collection of letters to include those covering Jefferson's conception and planning of the expedition, his close attention to its execution, and his later efforts to get the journals into print, I would have a project with a beginning, middle, and logical ending.

I decided to tackle first a substantial article on the subject, not only to discover the intensity of my interest but to demonstrate to the many persons with whom I must deal that I was capable of doing creditable work. In the summer of 1958 I worked on an article called "Some Books Carried by Lewis and Clark," a task made possible by the vast holdings of the University of Illinois Library, where I even found such rarities as the 1764 London edition of the *Dictionary of the Arts and Sciences*, a four-volume encyclopedia which I was able to establish as the set carried by the explorers. I submitted the article to the Missouri Historical Society at St. Louis, and it was published in the *Bulletin* of the society (October 1959).

Now I was rolling. In the fall of 1958 I wrote a memorandum to myself which, like all letters and memoranda cited or quoted here, is still in my files.

CORRESPONDENCE OF THE LEWIS AND CLARK EXPEDITION

11-16/58

An edition of all ltrs pertaining to the expedition and to the production of the original Biddle ed. and transfer of the jls to Am. Phil. Soc.

Published sources:
Thwaites
Coues
Nasatir
Writings of Jeff.
Ordway ltrs, see files
Pryor-Clark ltrs in AMHist. Rev.
Terr. Papers (for return of Sheheke, etc.)
Ltr to Sgt. Floyd's parents

Unpublished sources:
Biddle ltrs
Jefferson ltrs
NYPL Hassler
St. Louis: Mo. Hist. Soc.
Loos dissertation

Huntington has one

DeVoto Collection
Write the Hammond attorney
See if any ltrs in Minnesota notebooks
David Thompson from M. Lewis. Copy in Mo. Hist. Soc.
Procedure:
Go through Thwaites and catalog basic ltrs there. Then ck against Coues and Loos. It would be necessary to see Biddle coll. and those at Philadelphia. . . .

Pictures and maps
Biblio. All eds. of jls, plus works cited.
Get Thwaites microfilmed, then have it run off on paper at Ann Arbor.
Proofread ltrs in Thwaites against the originals. We have Jeff. microfilm.
Can you work in re Coues and Thwaites editorial work in intro. quoting from Coues ltrs to Harper etc?

The memorandum itself cries out for annotation, but that seems inappropriate here. The student of Lewis and Clark will perceive that I had already done some homework but had mapped trails that did not exist as I set off in the footsteps of the explorers. I correctly understood that two of my major sources of documents would be the Jefferson Papers at the Library of Congress and the Lewis and Clark collections at the Missouri Historical Society. In not listing the National Archives I was probably just taking that vast repository for granted, knowing that it had to be included in my search.

The problem of obtaining copies of all these docments did not seem to worry me but was to prove most difficult. We were in the age of the photostat, with xerography still in the developmental stage. My brave talk about having the eight-volume Thwaites edition "run off on paper" was wishful thinking, not only in terms of expense but of practicability. The process called Copy-Flo, the large-scale transfer of microfilm images to paper on a continuous web or roll, was not yet in general use. And certainly the days were far in the future when a researcher at a library or archive might casually stroll over to a copying machine in a corner of the reading room, insert a dime, and produce a copy to take home for more careful study.

As I review the letters I wrote and received while getting my Lewis and Clark search in gear, I am reminded that—although I was not a novice at scholarly writing and had already produced that fairly simple edition of Black Hawk's recollections—I was still not completely aware of the differences between editing a major collection of documents and producing a monograph based on those same materials. In the end I was to decide there were more similarities than differences.

Once a scholar decides that a project is worth doing, and believes that he or she can sustain the visceral fire needed to complete it, some questions come to mind that can be agonizing. Has this subject been dealt with before? If not, how am I to find out if there is a work in process? And how can I make an inquiry so ambiguously worded that I do not stimulate some other scholar—especially one who has done some spadework and needs only such an inquiry to galvanize him. This last question hardly seems praiseworthy, but young researchers can be as paranoid as anyone.

A famous student of western American history was notorious for always being at the point of starting any project about which a young student might query him. He also liked to assert his territorial imperative subtly by dropping into an article a footnote which might read: "The present writer now has a work in progress on this aspect of the subject" or "The papers of John Doe are soon to be edited and published by this writer."

An extreme example of manger-guarding is that of a scholar who writes a dissertation, then announces that he is expanding and revising it for publication. He has staked his claim, and no other scholar dares invest time and energy on untilled ground that may need desperately to be cultivated. A whole generation of historians may come and go, leaving a vital topic untouched.

Although today there is more communication among scholars, more lists of dissertations in progress and a few data bases available by computer, there is as yet no sure-fire way for a writer to discover whether or not he has a clear field. The best bet: write not only to librarians and archivists whose collections cover the subject and who are aware of the use being made of those collections, but also to other scholars who have recently published in the same area.

This ploy may not suffice. Once I worked for six months on the Red River Expedition of 1806, only to learn that Professor Dan Flores had signed a contract for a work on that identical subject with a university press. No one was to blame; the system had failed.

I surely would have consulted Bernard DeVoto had he still been living. I had met him as an undergraduate in 1942, under circumstances that he would have recalled, and he probably would have saluted my undertaking. I decided instead to approach John Bakeless, whose *Lewis and Clark: Partners in Discovery* was a joint biography of the explorers based on such manuscript sources as were known in the 1940s.

Dear Professor Bakeless: January 19, 1959
    We would value your advice about a Lewis and Clark project that we may undertake here at the University Press. Your own book on the explorers is, of course, the Compleat Lewis and Clark, and our high opinion of that work leads us to seek your opinion first of all. May I add that I know your *Tragicall History* of Marlowe well, and am happy to find it cited often in a Shakespearean work by T. W. Baldwin that we are now publishing.
    About a year ago it occurred to me that the correspondence generated by the Lewis and Clark expedition is quite scattered; and I noted during trips to St. Louis and to the old army section of the National Archives that a good bit of the material is unpublished. So I set out to calendar all the Lewis and Clark correspondence I could find. I wound up with a listing of 270 letters— some of them, naturally, unimportant. . . . The published letters are scattered throughout twenty works, with Thwaites having the biggest share (74) in his appendix to the *Journals.* But Thwaites did not annotate the letters very carefully, he did not transcribe them accurately, and his edition is getting scarcer every day. To summarize: the total correspondence of the expedition is not readily available, and it ought to be compiled and edited in a single volume.

Continuing, I developed for Bakeless the nature of my proposal, told him something of my background, and mentioned my forthcoming article in the *Bulletin* of the Missouri Historical Society. In other words, I touched all the bases: fawned shamelessly on the man, outlined my proposal, and made sure he knew that I was capable of being published in a reputable journal. I even enlisted the prestige of the University of Illinois Press by claiming that the work might be issued there, although this was by no means certain.

The response by Bakeless on 22 January was exactly what I needed to urge me on. "It would certainly serve scholarship," he said, "to issue the collection of letters you propose. It would have been a godsend to me some years ago." He then mentioned some specific letters and documents he hoped I would not overlook, and said, "You must know all about the Minnesota papers"—which fortunately I did. "Doubtless you have thought of following up BPC and ABPC, which I have often found revealing." I discovered he was referring to *Book Prices Current* and *American Book Prices Current*, where books and manuscripts sold at auction are compiled and listed annually.

Bakeless sent his regards to Quincy Howe (visiting faculty) and Marcus and Agnes Goldman (faculty), and "to that good and great man T. W. B!" My reference to his work on Marlowe sent him off into a fond recollection: "I was first shown Sir John Squires' review of the *Tragicall History* on Mount Pelion in 1944, by a Seafarth Highlander, who, like myself, was 'up to no good' for the German Army, who completely surrounded us. Book reviews do turn up in the damnedest places!"

With no delay at all, I wrote on 26 January to Charles van Ravenswaay, director of the Missouri Historical Society, whose assent was essential to my plans. The Lewis and Clark holdings of the society were substantial and essential. For a scholar to go to a collection and do extensive work in it is natural and desirable; it is why such collections, public and private, are established. But when the scholar asks if he may publish an entire collection verbatim, a quite different question arises. Such societies as the one in St. Louis owe their existence to the visitations of scholars, but when their collections are put into print the visitations are reduced. Boards of directors grow restive. Corporations and wealthy private supporters grow restive. Annual reports are more carefully and more inventively phrased, as attendance in the reading rooms drops.

This problem of archivists, in an age when the publication of documentary editions is expanding, was made clear to me a decade later when I had just been appointed editor of the newly established *Papers of George Washington* at the University of Virginia. I had asked James Thorpe, director of the Henry E. Huntington Library and Art Gallery, for permission to copy and later publish the Huntington's substantial collection of Washington documents. Already knowing of the project, no doubt he considered my appearance in his office inevitable and the force behind my request inexorable. He gave his immediate consent—but with some regret. "You are wiping us out," he said. "When your edition begins to appear, we will no longer be the resource for George Washington scholars that we are today. Still, we yield to the inescapable fact that you are making our materials more easily accessible to a greater number of users."

I feel sure that the same kind of chill brushed across van Ravenswaay's brow the morning he received my letter, partially quoted here:

Dear Mr. van Ravenswaay: January 26, 1959

This University Press is now considering the advisability of compiling and editing the correspondence generated by the Lewis and Clark Expedition. The purpose of this letter is to ask for permission to include in our collection the pertinent material in your archives.

As you know, the letters of the expedition are rather scattered. Many of the more basic ones have been published, in the appendix to the Thwaites *Journals* and elsewhere, but they are not well annotated and are in many cases poorly transcribed. A substantial number of letters remains unpublished. These are housed mainly in the Library of Congress, National Archives, Missouri Historical Society, and American Philosophical Society. It seems to us that we could serve the cause of Lewis and Clark scholarship by making all this material available in a single volume with appropriate annotation.

The work of compiling and editing would be done by Professor Donald Jackson, editor of the Press. He is an experienced student of the period, has other publications in progress, and has worked from time to time in your own archives. He has an article forthcoming in the October issue of your *Bulletin....* Dr. Jackson has been in contact with John Bakeless, whom I am sure you know ... and Mr. Bakeless has expressed great interest in the project as well as a willingness to advise us as needed.... I want to assure you that this undertaking will be handled in a thorough, scholarly manner, and that we shall try hard to make it a credit to the great historical enterprise it seeks to illuminate.

The letter, drafted by me, was signed by the late Miodrag Muntyan, director of the press. As my project depended entirely on the consent of van Ravenswaay, I had played my trump card by using my friend Mid Muntyan's name and title. We had van Ravenswaay's response of 29 January in hand before I had long to fret about his possible refusal: "The plan outlined in your letter of January 26 for publishing the correspondence generated by the Lewis and Clark expedition seems to me an excellent and long needed one, and this Society would be happy to cooperate and to make available its manuscript materials. When Dr. Jackson plans to visit us, please ask that he contact our

Manuscript Librarian, Mrs. Ernst A. Stadler, who will be happy to assist him."

Now I was ready to approach the dean of documentary editing and, in the process, to commit a blunder that must have seemed more inept to him than to me. At Princeton University, Julian P. Boyd was editing the *Papers of Thomas Jefferson,* a task he had undertaken about a decade earlier. He had published fifteen volumes and had established an editorial method which was, with modification, to become the standard for documentary editors of our generation. His approbation would have been important to me for this reason alone, and because I knew him to be a devotee of anything pertaining to Lewis and Clark, but primarily because so many of the documents I wished to publish were letters to and from Jefferson. Although most of the Jefferson letters were in archives in the public domain, such as the Library of Congress and the National Archives, a halfhearted assent from Boyd would have hampered me, if only psychologically. So I put my best foot forward, or so I thought, and wrote him.

Dear Dr. Boyd: February 9, 1959
    This Press is planning to undertake a publishing venture which overlaps *The Papers of Thomas Jefferson* slightly. We need your advice and your help.
    We hope to compile and edit the correspondence generated by the Lewis and Clark Expedition. By our present estimates, somewhat more than half of it has been published—in scattered sources. . . . We feel that the unpublished letters and documents are sufficiently important, and the published ones sufficiently hard to obtain, that we can perform a service by pulling all the material into one volume. The Missouri Historical Society has given us access to their fine Lewis and Clark collection.
    Because of Jefferson's involvement with the expedition, it is readily apparent that many of his letters must be included. My preliminary checklist contains 109 letters either to or from Jefferson, and I am sure there are others; many deal but briefly with the expedition and should not be used intact. . . .
    Is it possible that your TJ Editorial File now has transcripts of all or part of these letters, and that these could be made available to us? There are obvious advantages to the public in issuing standard versions of these letters; but of course our real motive is a saving of time and funds which we could then apply to the rest of the Lewis and Clark material.
    I realize first of all that you may not have transcribed so far in advance of your publication schedule. Also, that other researchers may have plagued you with similar requests until you have had to decline them all. . . . Suppose you cannot make transcripts available. Could you lend us paper prints such as those Lyman Butterfield speaks of in the *American Archivist,* XII (1949)

134? The cost of enlarged reproductions from microfilm, done here in our university photo laboratory, is very high.

Boyd's reply arrived promptly:

Dear Mr. Jackson: February 11, 1959
I have read your letter with much interest and of course will be glad to talk with you at any time you happen to come this way, even though I doubt if I could be very helpful in your editorial problems. I am interested to learn that you plan a volume of the letters, though I would have been happier if your plan had been for a really comprehensive edition [of Lewis and Clark writings]. This is what is urgently needed — and has been needed from the beginning.

As for duplication, I am not at all disturbed about this: the taxpayers of Illinois do not mind duplicating textbooks, test tubes, and basketballs in institutions of learning, so why should they mind duplicating the letters of the authors of our first epic journey of exploration? Nor would I insist on a standard form of presentation as between one edition and another: each has its different needs to meet and these *may* dictate different forms.

But I wish it were possible for me to accommodate you by making our materials available. Unfortunately to do so in one case would impose upon us the obligation of doing so in all cases, and for this reason the Editorial Committee in the beginning of the enterprise laid down the policy that our files could not be opened for research purposes, since to do so would make it literally impossible for us to meet publication schedules and to discharge our primary task as an editorial undertaking.

However, in order to assist scholars in their researches and to make more accessible to them while our edition is in progress such Jefferson documents as we have accumulated, we have microfilmed all our control files. These files consist of chronological, alphabetical (by name of author and recipient only), and bibliographical cards giving the identification and location of approximately 60,000 letters by and to Thomas Jefferson and other documents. . . . Seven copies of this film have been presented to libraries on condition that they would be available on interlibrary loan.

In retrospect, I see that I was bothered about the wrong thing in Boyd's letter. I felt embarrassed at my naive assumption — even so tentatively stated — that he might provide me with transcripts or photocopies. He was absolutely correct in this firm refusal, as I was to learn a decade later when I was trying to get more than 100,000 George Washington letters under control at the University of Virginia and was showered with requests from researchers. What should have given me greater pause was his assertion that a complete new edition of the journals and all related materials was urgently needed. His instinct was correct, and today a new edition of the journals is being edited by Dr. Gary N. Moulton at the

University of Nebraska. But an edition of that scope was far beyond my means and plans in 1959 (and Boyd later would tell me he was satisfied with my decision to do only the letters, and give them the emphasis they might not have received in a more comprehensive edition of Lewis and Clark materials.

It now seemed that I was beyond the stage of marking out my territory and alerting the scholarly community that I was open for business. Collecting documents was the next step. It should not be supposed, however, that these "steps" fell into any kind of rigid order. Documentary editing is no different from other manuscript preparation: I read voraciously in the Lewis and Clark literature; I enlarged my bibliography of books and articles still to be read; I cranked twice through the Library of Congress microfilm edition of the Thomas Jefferson Papers; I made stacks of note cards and filed them without any way of knowing if they would serve me later; I kept an eye out for suitable illustrations and maps; and I pursued my interest in finding an off-campus publisher, preferably a trade publisher, despite the willingness of our own editorial committee to approve the work for publication by the press.

My need to travel and to obtain microfilm and other copies might have hindered me if my superiors and the staff of the university library had not been generous. Although I held academic rank as an associate professor at that time, I was a year-round faculty member with a month's vacation, expected to keep regular office hours and to travel only on university business.

I managed the travel by using vacation time, and sometimes by slipping in an extra day of research while manning the press's exhibit table at professional meetings. The library did not hesitate to order such standard items as the letters to and from the Secretary of War, a set of microfilm reels issued by the National Archives. The Research Board of the Graduate College loaned me a Recordak microfilm reader originally purchased for the use of another faculty member. In looking back at the repositories that I called upon personally, and the materials for research that came my way, I must conclude that I was given as much freedom as I needed—as long as I kept the wheels turning at the press.

I had worked in Washington, D.C., on earlier projects and knew the routines. I recall with pleasure those days at the National Archives when a searcher was permitted to go into reading areas within the stacks and virtually take up residence there, consulting specialists and, if necessary, going into the stack areas to rummage personally—under supervision—in the treasures of that great establishment. Sara Dunlap Jackson, revered by any researcher who has worked at the Archives within the past thirty years, was one of the first to shepherd me through the labyrinths in the 1950s.

The ambience at the Library of Congress was more austere, although friends could be made there, too, including manuscript librarian David C. Mearns. The security system, much more rigid at that time than the system at the Archives, closed around me one afternoon like a police ambush. I had carelessly brought with me into the reading room a rare book just purchased at Lowdermilk's, and at checkout time the guard's eye fell upon the wrapped parcel. I was escorted to the "captain's" office, where the chief of security watched as I unwrapped the book and persuaded him that it was my own. The parcel had been wrapped for mailing home on my way back to the hotel, and the imperious guard would neither help me rewrap it nor direct me to a source of gummed tape and other wrapping supplies.

The old Francis Scott Key Hotel was in those days the place for academics with limited funds. It provided kitchenettes and Murphy-bed rooms to a clientele that also included families called to foreign service who had come to Washington for briefing and transportation overseas. The entranceway was always stacked with footlockers marked for transshipment.

In the summer of 1959 I went first to the library of the American Philosophical Society, in Philadelphia, and then on to Washington. At the National Archives I looked up two persons who had been recommended to me by John Francis McDermott, of St. Louis, and in doing so I found myself involved in questioning no less penetrating than that applied to a Ph.D. candidate undergoing his oral examination. The two men I called on were Oliver W. Holmes, chief archivist of the Social and Economic Records Division of the National Archives, and Herman R. Friis, chief archivist of the Cartographic Records Division. This pair had recently been involved as expert witnesses in an unsuccessful suit brought by the government to recover recently identified William Clark field notes from a private owner in St. Paul, Minnesota, on the grounds that the documents were produced while Clark was in public service.

Holmes and Friis invited me to lunch, and I soon realized that I was undergoing a searching look at my qualifications to edit the Lewis and Clark letters. They must have concluded that I was sufficiently prepared; I have often reflected that my luncheon with those two, later to become my fast friends, was my final initiation into the fraternity of Lewis and Clark scholar-buffs.

In the fall of 1959 I received my only nibble from a trade publisher. I had sent a query to the book-review section of the *New York Times*, the kind used to fill space at the end of a column, asking for Lewis and Clark documents. My response from holders of manuscripts was a disappointment, but I did receive a letter from Mrs. G. D. de Santillana of the Houghton Mifflin Company in Boston. She would be interested in learning more about my project. As this respected firm had published DeVoto's edition of the Lewis and Clark journals a few years earlier, I entered into correspondence with Mrs. de Santillana, managing editor, and later with Craig Wylie, who was important enough not to put his title on his letters. I sent them sample documents with footnotes, and for a while I had high hopes. Eventually I received a final rejection from Mr. Wylie, and that ended my relationship with Houghton Mifflin for more than twenty years, when a novel of mine was selected for publication by Ticknor & Fields, a subsidiary.

I was now well into the collecting phase of the work. A document that almost eluded me was the subject of a long search and a sticky problem of permission to publish. John Bakeless had told me of a notation on the cover of a Clark account book, ca. 1825–28, in which Clark had set down the names of as many members of the expedition as he could recall, and noted what had happened to them. Of special interest was his listing the Shoshoni girl Sacagawea as dead by that time, contradicting another theory that she lived to be a very old woman on the Wind River reservation in Wyoming. Unfortunately Bakeless did not know who owned the document, which had not been available when he published his biography of the explorers in 1947.

In the fall of 1959 I had sent inquiries to several depositories, having traced the sale of the account book in 1941 as reported in *American Book Prices Current.* In October I sent a routine inquiry to Everett D. Graff, a private collector in Illinois, asking in a general way about his holdings. He replied that he could not think of anything he owned that would be suitable for my edition.

By December, however, I had learned from a now-forgotten source that Graff owned the Clark account book and had placed it on deposit at the Newberry Library in Chicago. I seem to recall that Graff was in the process of giving his entire collection to the Newberry in installments, undoubtedly to maximize their value to him as a tax deduction. I quickly sent off an inquiry to Graff about using the document, and received from Colton Storm, a curator at the Newberry, this disappointing reply:

The University of Illinois Press

is pleased to send you a review copy of

Among the Sleeping Giants
Occasional Pieces on Lewis and Clark

Donald Jackson
With a foreword by Savoie Lottinville

Publication date: December 16, 1987

Price: $17.95

We would appreciate two copies of any published review.

UNIVERSITY OF ILLINOIS PRESS
54 East Gregory Drive, Champaign, IL 61820

Dear Mr. Jackson: 19 January 1960
    Mr. Graff has given me your letter of November 28 to him and has asked
me to reply to it.
    I can both applaud and deplore Mr. Graff's decision that he does not wish
you to use the Clark account book. Since his collection is coming gradually
to the Newberry Library, I can cheer for the unpublished character of the
materials which will someday be at the service of readers in the library. Few
things are more welcome to a librarian than unused resources.
    On the other hand, it seems a pity that you, working toward publication,
should be deprived of source material. . . . This, I am certain you understand,
I deplore.

I did not press the matter for several months. Near the end of the year I
had another exchange with Storm, and he wrote me in early December
that Graff was still adamant. But two months later, for reasons I am not
aware of, Graff relented and Storm wrote me:

Dear Mr. Jackson   22 February 1961
    I don't know whether or not this will come as a pleasurable surprise, but I
hope it does. Mr. Graff has reconsidered the matter of the William Clark
document on the cover of his account book about 1828 and has decided that
you may publish the text from the photograph which you now have. We
assume that you will send us a copy of the text and your comments before
the work is sent to press.
    Personally, I am delighted that the affair has turned out this way.

The elusive Clark doodle became item No. 404a in my edition and did
much to put to rest the assertions of Grace Raymond Hebard, whose
Sacajawea, a Guide and Interpreter of the Lewis and Clark Expedition
(Glendale, Calif., 1933), about the identity of the old woman on the
Wind River reservation claiming to be Sacagawea, was widely believed.
It is now generally accepted that Sacagawea died at Fort Clark, on the
Upper Missouri, in December 1812.
    I learned from this experience that private collectors must be approached
with much circumspection and with guarded hope. Some fear the mone-
tary value of their holdings will be reduced by publication, although I
have never believed this was true in most cases. Others are motivated by
the usually erroneous belief that their holdings—such as an ancestor's
Civil War letters—might bring forth handsome royalties when published.
But the most difficult of all collectors are those whose pride of ownership
motivates their acquisition of rare items.
    A woman in St. Louis had intimated to scholars that she owned a
number of Lewis and Clark items when I was at work on my edition, but

I knew of only one that was in her possession for certain. It was a letter of 15 April 1803 from Meriwether Lewis to General William Irvine, superintendent of military stores in Philadelphia, regarding the portable or condensed soup that Lewis wished to carry on the expedition. She firmly denied me access to this letter, which after her death became the property of a public archive and proved to be a minor item. It was the only original manuscript she owned. According to custom, she had a right to withhold it from publication because of her ownership, although if I had found Lewis's retained copy I could have published it with impunity, as he had written it in an official capacity and it was thus in the public domain. I was eventually to learn that the owner was fiercely protective of Lewis's memory. She had done a master's thesis on an aspect of his post-expedition life and was, I believe, working on a book at the time of her death.

In May 1960 I began what my family came to call my Vardis Fisher experience, extending over a period of two years. The late Mr. Fisher, a novelist living in Idaho, whose best-known work was his "Testament of Man" series including such titles as *Darkness and the Deep, The Golden Rooms,* and *Adam and the Serpent,* had published a fictitious account of the Lewis and Clark Expedition, *Tale of Valor,* and was deeply caught up in the question of how Lewis met his death.

At that time it was commonly believed that the former explorer, then governor of Upper Louisiana, had been murdered at a tavern along the Natchez Trace in Tennessee, while traveling to Washington in the late summer of 1809. This theory had been supported by Elliott Coues and others, and more recently by Bakeless. But a single article by Dawson A. Phelps in the *William and Mary Quarterly* (July 1956) had reintroduced the original belief about Lewis's death, embraced by Jefferson and by William Clark, that Lewis had taken his own life. My own study of the documents, and the cogency of Phelps's arguments, had persuaded me to adopt the suicide theory as highly tenable.

Vardis Fisher wrote that he had been working for the past two and a half years on the death of Lewis, and had only to go once more to the Natchez Trace region before completing the manuscript. In the belief that Jefferson might have left a memorandum on the subject more specific than his published statement in a memoir of Lewis, Fisher had written to Julian Boyd, asking permission "to examine the unedited Jefferson papers for the last months of 1809." Boyd had declined, but Fisher — believing incorrectly that I already had been given access to Boyd's files — inquired if I knew of such a memorandum. He also said he had sent seven questions to my reluctant St. Louis correspondent. "She wrote that she could answer a number of them but did not feel that doing so would be to her own best interests."

We made plans for Fisher to visit me in October, an arrangement that did not materialize. In midsummer I sent him a transcribed document I had received from the Eli Lilly Library at Indiana University that was among the papers of Jonathan Williams, the first superintendent of the U.S. Military Academy. I added this comment to my covering letter: "It occurs to me that I don't know whether your forthcoming book on Lewis's death is a novel or a factual account. At any rate, I know you want to see all the documentary material." The manuscript I sent him was a statement by Captain Gilbert Russell bearing on the mental and physical condition of Lewis when he stopped at Chickasaw Bluffs (now Memphis), on his fatal trek to Washington. It was damaging testimony concerning Lewis's alcoholism.

Fisher's reply of 9 July told me for the first time that he was a proponent of the murder theory. "It is no exaggeration to say that your letter of 6 July and transcription of the document were a bombshell in my life. I read half the first page and was so astonished that I went back and reread, knowing that if this is authentic it overthrows my thesis that Lewis did not kill himself." He added that indeed he was writing a factual account of the episode, not a fictionalized one.

Instead of accepting the Russell document, Fisher fought it. "Somewhere early in the second page I was strongly feeling that Gilbert Russell never wrote this, and by the time I reached the end of it I was convinced that he did not." He thus set the tone for the exchanges that were to follow. He was behaving not so much as a historian but as a special investigator who had put himself on a case and was going after the perpetrator. Thus he not only questioned the content of the manuscript but the authenticity of the document itself. I replied that "I have no reason to doubt the authenticity of the Russell statement, and I think it is a truthful account of what Russell understood the facts to be."

"The unhappy fact is," Fisher responded, "that if the letter attributed to Russell is genuine I may not have a book. I respect your belief that it is. . . . Your present opinion that Lewis killed himself I also respect but cannot share, not yet. I may have to."

It was inevitable that Fisher would ask me to read his manuscript and that I would agree. During the summer I prepared eight single-spaced pages of remarks and criticisms, hammering away on the following themes:

His refusal to believe that "a man like Lewis" could be a courageous explorer and fine military man and still be brought to the point of self-destruction by the circumstances of life and the machinations of his mind. His manipulation of evidence. His reliance on oral tradition, even when it conflicted with the story told by contemporary documents. His emphasis on negative evidence: why didn't Agent Neelly do this, why didn't tavern-keeper Mrs. Grinder do that? His approach to the whole problem not as a historian but as a Holmesian detective with all the principal characters dead, no eyewitnesses, the scene of the occurrence obliterated.

After some revision in which Fisher reluctantly adjusted his approach while retaining strong leanings toward the murder theory, his book was published as *Suicide or Murder? The Strange Death of Meriwether Lewis* (Denver, 1962).

It is easy to criticize Fisher without understanding his dilemma. He was basically a storyteller and the murder of Lewis was his story line for a great new narrative. But this was history, not a novel, and he was not able to let his imagination range free; the contemporary testimony and sparse evidence kept getting in the way, and he had difficulty in accepting them. He did what my navy drill instruction in boot camp would have called "Right face . . . hup!" A full about-face would have been better, or even an orderly retirement from the drill field.

On my second trip to the East Coast in the summer of 1960 I went as a known quantity. The archivists I saw were acquaintances or at least correspondents, and some already were friends. I took them copies of documents I had found during the year and they gave me new material. During the trip I discovered one letter from Lewis to Jefferson, with an enclosure, that had become separated into four parts and lodged in three different repositories. Two of the missing parts were in the Massachusetts Historical Society but in different files. When reassembled, the letter enabled me to identify a new Lewis and Clark map, the first that Clark prepared upon taking up residence for the winter on the Illinois side of the Mississippi in 1804–5.

By now I was becoming an expert at transcribing manuscripts into typescript, a chore that I have never felt should be left to a willing secretary or graduate student, for an accurate transcription is the vital core of a documentary editor's work. In learning to transcribe I had also learned to identify the handwriting of such diverse penmen as Lewis, Clark, Jefferson, dozens of their correspondents, and the curious, intense hand of Nicholas Biddle.

Biddle was a well-known figure in Philadelphia literary, political, and financial circles who, after Lewis's death, had been persuaded by Clark to write a narrative of the expedition. I have always thought it surprised Lewis and Clark greatly to learn that the neat journals they brought back from the expedition were not acceptable to publishers exactly as written. Lewis was believed to be working on a new version at the time of his death, though it now appears that his failure to deliver a manuscript was a mental burden that may have contributed to his suicide. In any case, no revised manuscript has been found. It fell upon Clark, no literary man, to find a collaborator who could put the journals into some kind of publishable form. By the spring of 1810 he had persuaded Nicholas Biddle to undertake the task, and enough correspondence had ensued for me to have developed a good feel for the almost illegible Biddle hand.

At the American Philosophical Society, leafing through the notebook in which Lewis had penned his journal during a descent of the Ohio River in 1803, I came across many pages in a strange hand. Apparently no one had recognized the hand before, not even Milo Milton Quaife when he edited the Lewis journal for publication in 1916. Slowly it came to me that this was Biddle's hand, and that Biddle had used blank pages in Lewis's journal to set down notes on the expedition during a visit to Clark at Fincastle, Virginia, in 1810.

An anxiously awaited microfilm copy enabled me to spend many weeks after my return laboriously transcribing what came to be known as the "Biddle notes," and which appear on pp. 1:497–545 of my *Letters*. Although these notes proved to be among the most valuable contributions in my edition, one captious reviewer, who had compared my transcription with the original and found a minor misreading, used the occasion to point out the shortcomings of working from microfilm. Holy mackerel! He ought to have praised the development of a technique that enabled me to spend weeks at a task that I never could have accomplished had I been required to stay in Philadelphia and work from the original.

In the spring of 1960 I traveled by car with my wife Cathie and two young sons, Robert and Mark, to Boston, Philadelphia, Washington, and Charlottesville, Virginia. As we drove through the streets of Charlottesville and made a long-awaited visit to Jefferson's Monticello, we were of one mind: the town was interesting and rather quaint, but no place for a family from the Cornbelt to want to live. Eight years later I was to be looking for housing there in my new capacity as founding editor of *The Papers of George Washington*.

As I made my way about the country visiting repositories, I became more and more convinced there was no substitute for personal inspection of collections. To write a librarian and ask "Is there anything in the Smith collection on the Lewis and Clark Expedition?" is, first, to impose upon a very busy and probably understaffed institution. It is also to risk missing something consequential, and not just because the person assigned to the search may be careless. Documents about events such as an expedition, in which many persons are involved, may not contain clear indications of their meaning that can be discovered by scanning. The expedition may not be mentioned because the correspondents know well what they have been writing about. The letter may have content that might illuminate an aspect of the subject in a footnote; only in the mind of the editor does it immediately appear as something of value. As my experience grew, I developed a mental list of persons whose correspondence should never be overlooked, even if carefully cataloged with no mention of Lewis and Clark in the summary of contents.

Uncataloged collections were an even more difficult matter. The holdings of the National Archives are so vast that they can only be arranged into "record groups" and certain subgroupings. Consider the collection called "Muster, pay, and recruiting rolls, First Infantry Regiment, 1802–1811, Record Group 94." No doubt by now those records have been laminated and put into some order, but in 1960 they were tattered, crumbling, and not to be handled by a researcher whose care with documents had not been observed by an archivist. I obtained much information about the enlisted men of Lewis and Clark from these records. Another incredibly difficult group were the financial accounts of the U.S. army, housed in a hot warehouse across town; yet they were essential in piecing together the total cost of the expedition.

In reviewing my correspondence of the period, I am struck by a strange omission. Most of the letters I wrote were about the existence or nonexistence of documents, and my arrangements for obtaining copies or traveling to see them. There are no letters about the editorial process. I knew of no other beginner who was doing anything similar to my project, and I was reluctant to write to the obviously experienced ones. What a wealth of learning I might have obtained, and what long hours of trial and error I might have avoided, had I been as bold about asking Boyd for advice on textual problems and matters of annotation as I had been in asking for copies of his documents.

Being self-taught has the advantage of encouraging one to be innovative through ignorance, on the one hand, and watchful for standard practices on the other. When I had finished my manuscript, I had amassed enough on-the-job experience so that I probably could have showered a novice with editorial homilies.

It pleased me to know that, in a large manuscript containing only a few lines of the famous Lewis and Clark journals, I had told the story of the trek, its beginnings and its aftermath, in a new way. As I riffled the pages, there was Jefferson's letter to General James Wilkinson, in February 1801, ordering his young friend Lewis released from duty on the Ohio so that he could become the President's personal secretary. An alert from the Spanish minister in Philadelphia to his superiors, warning them of the impending intrusion into Louisiana. The secret cipher that Jefferson and Lewis had worked out, if needed to communicate from deep in the West. Lewis's British and French passports, the first obtained from the Archivo General de Indias in Seville and the second from an old photostat in the Library of Congress. Dr. Benjamin Rush's rules of health for the explorers ("Flannel should be worn constantly next to the skin, especially in wet weather"). Lewis writing to Clark in June 1803, asking if he would be interested in voyaging to the Pacific, and Clark's enthusiastic reply. Jefferson's detailed instructions to Lewis, showing the depth of his involvement in the enterprise. The list of marvels—plant and animal specimens, Indian artifacts—being sent back from the Mandan villages in the spring of 1805. The triumphant letter to Jefferson a year and a half later when the expedition returned to St. Louis. Lewis's letter to the Secretary of War, appraising the performance of each enlisted man and civilian in the party. And, of course, the hundreds of notes that had cost me so many nights and Sundays.

The work, containing 428 documents occupying 728 pages, was published in the spring of 1962, reprinted with minor corrections in 1963, and later published in a two-volume second edition in 1978. Not many authors or documentary editors have the privilege of babying a favorite manuscript through the publishing process. My position at the press required me to solicit from book manufacturers across the country for the typesetting and binding of the edition, which meant choosing the paper, type, and binding cloth with the concurrence of the designer. In this case the designer was also a mentor, for Carroll Coleman—hired to design the book as a freelancer—had taught me to set type by hand in 1947 and 1948 at the University of Iowa. He was an "old school" printer from whom Gutenberg could have learned, and he remains my cherished friend to this day.

Carroll and I were disheartened when the manufacturer, a well-known firm on the East Coast, gave the work to a typesetter who did not follow instructions: close spacing, using thin Linotype spacebands, with no extra space between sentences. The result was a loosely set book, with ugly rivers of white space meandering down across the pages. Had I been an off-campus author I might have had to live with that atrocity, for it takes nerve even for a publisher to insist that a book be entirely reset in a workmanlike manner. Again backed by Director Muntyan, I told the printer just that, and redoing the galleys probably cost him his entire profit on the job.

The result, however, was worth the effort to us, for the volume was chosen as one of the Fifty Books of the Year by the American Institute of Graphic Arts. The errant printer took part of the credit, as he should have, and my career as two kinds of editor began to jell.

Lewis and Clark Place-Names in Montana

*F*rom the Snowy Mountains of eastern Australia the Murray River flows west for nearly 2,000 miles, joined along the way by the Mitta Mitta, the Ovens, the Goulburn, the Campaspe, the Lodden, the Murrumbidgee, and the Darling rivers. Who can hear or read of these remote watercourses without wanting to know where the names came from and what they can tell us?

Around the world, the way that a tribe, community, or nation decides on names for its geographic places has become a useful line of inquiry in such fields as history, geography, sociology, and folklore studies. It has not been widely employed in the study of American exploration, however, despite what it can tell us about the cultural setting for an expedition, the personal background of its members, and the national aims of those who have made discoveries on the North American continent.

In a limited way I have undertaken to apply the study of place-names — also called toponymy — to a particular U.S. exploration, and to show how such names have been treated by generations of migrants that followed.

A party of explorers merely accelerates the naming process as it moves across an unknown territory. Later, wandering trappers, surveyors for a railroad, or a wagon train of settlers seeking new homes may reject or accept the explorers' names and apply new ones, but the process is the same. The naming of streams, mountains, and eventually inhabited places may go at a slower pace as a territory is developed later, but there is always a moment in time when a name is chosen, either by one person or a group, and left to fend for itself.

Place-naming involves cartography, often a bit of genealogy, and always the several disciplines of historical and linguistic research. The reader who expects more cartographic study, for example, than my topic requires will be disappointed. So will the reader who hopes for a complete retelling of the oft-told Lewis and Clark epic.

In their journey to the Pacific Northwest in 1804–6, Meriwether Lewis and William Clark were charged by President Thomas Jefferson with exacting tasks. They were to make maps of a vast area, study its natural history and its native peoples, and find a passage across the Rocky Mountains to the mouth of the Columbia River. Nowhere in Jefferson's painstakingly drafted instructions was there a line about one of the most onerous of assignments, seemingly taken for granted. In charting a passage up the Missouri River, across the mountains, and down the watercourses flowing to the Pacific, Lewis and Clark were expected to assign a name to every river and creek, butte, peak, or other significant topographic feature.

Aids to place-naming were available in a few maps and journals of earlier travelers. The Missouri River from its mouth to the Mandan villages of present North Dakota had been mapped and described by men interested in French trade with the Indians. On the Pacific coast the British, French, Russians, and Spaniards had mapped the coast and penetrated some distance inland, leaving a few names on maps that were spartan in style and few in number.

Most givers of place-names do so with no regard for previous or existing names, either out of ignorance or with knowing disregard. Lewis and Clark were careful to search out names already used by Indian tribes or earlier European travelers, and to use them on their maps. But often their scruples were overruled by the urge to innovate, and even more often they had no earlier names to rely upon. During two years of travel they were to record or invent hundreds of place-names. That their inventiveness and quest for novelty often overrode their sense of history will be seen in the following pages. It will also be apparent that in giving names to nearly dry creeks on the sweltering plains, amid the distractions of mosquito bites and prickly-pear thorns, they could be as dull as the landscape that confronted them.

This essay is concerned more with names than with places.

Place-Naming with Lewis and Clark

Every exploring team is likely to depend on two principal aids: maps of earlier travels, accurate or fanciful; and guides who know something of the country and whatever names have already been assigned to it. For the eastern and western ends of their route, Lewis and Clark had both maps and live guides of uneven usefulness. For the great, mysterious midroute — reaching across the Upper Plains and the Rocky Mountains — they had neither.

The detailed planning for a trek across the continent might be said to have started with the publication of a journal and map of Alexander Mackenzie, who had traveled across Canada late in the eighteenth century. The implied threat of British domination in the Pacific Northwest so aroused Jefferson, already eager to explore the country, that in 1802 he began vigorous planning with his aide, Meriwether Lewis.

Starting with Mackenzie's *Voyages from Montreal,* Jefferson and Lewis began to assemble the sparse published maps and narratives of seafaring explorers who had cruised the Pacific coast from Baja California to the Bering Strait, and cartographers whose information was part conjecture, part fantasy. From these a compilation was made, so that Lewis and Clark could carry on one large sheet all that was known about the country west of the Mississippi.

When the exploring party, now joined by William Clark and made up primarily of American soldiers, had reached their staging ground near St. Louis, a particularly useful map was obtained by Jefferson and sent to them. James Mackay, a Scottish trader and explorer in the service of the Spanish government, had produced a map based in part on his own travels, extending from St. Louis to the villages of the Mandan and Hidatsa tribes in what is now North Dakota. When its French place-names were joined by English translations, the explorers had in hand a remarkably accurate and bilingual map covering the first 1,400 miles of their journey.

Although few of the French boatmen or *engagés* employed by Lewis and Clark would have presented themselves as "guides," most were qualified as such. They had plied the Missouri and its tributaries in search of beaver, their means of livelihood, had intermarried with women of the tribes, and had accumulated their own mingling of French and Indian names for topographic features along the way.

Lewis knew only a bit of French and Clark even less, and Clark's written English was not much more than adequate for a frontiersman of his day. As the mapmaker of the expedition, he was sorely tried by this handicap when the little flotilla (a large keelboat and smaller pirogues with about forty men) moved up the lower reaches of the Mississippi. The late John Francis McDermott, a student of the early Louisiana Territory who had been decorated as a scholar by the government of France, was amused and affronted by Clark's struggle to master the French place-names. It bothered him that the expedition's well-known winter camp opposite the mouth of the Missouri is now called Wood River instead of Wood's River, because Clark commonly rendered the French as *Rivière Dubois* instead of *Rivière à Dubois.* His Beef Island

and Beef River, named early on the trip, were erroneously derived from the French *boeuf,* which meant bison or buffalo to the French of the Mississippi Valley. And Shepherd's Creek was not known to the French as one frequented by a sheepherder or *berger,* but named for a man named Berger, thus *Rivière à Berger.* These are not grievous errors for a man who came from a society that could render *Bois Brulé* as Bob Ruly, and call the Purgatoire River of Colorado the Picketwire.

Clark gives us an attention-getting sample of how he proposes to spell his way across the Plains and Rockies when, on the first day out of Wood River, he writes in his journal that the expedition proceeded on "under a jentle brease." There is worse to come.

On the first leg of their journey, as they labored upstream for five months to reach the Mandan and Hidatsa villages, Lewis and Clark performed their place-naming chores even more circumspectly than might have been required. As they were representing the U.S. government, officially charting a portion of the Louisiana Purchase that had recently been obtained from France, they might have engaged in wholesale renaming of the old French and Indian toponyms. But they forebore. Gathering their information as correctly as possible, and spelling the names with aplomb if not always with accuracy, they moved up past Bonom (Bon Homme) Creek, Deavels Race Ground, Seeder Island, Luter (L'outre) Island, Grinestone Creek, Hay Cabbin Creek, and Turquie Creike (Turkey Creek).

Below the Mandan villages, the "official" narrative journal is in Clark's hand. Scholars are debating whether or not Lewis kept a conventional journal during this time, or only notes and other data, and the debate undoubtedly will go on unless a journal is found. A few other members of the expedition, literate enlisted men, kept their own journals. That of Sergeant John Ordway is the best and most complete. Sergeant Patrick Gass kept a record that survives only in a version reworked and published by a Pittsburgh bookseller. Private Joseph Whitehouse kept a journal, and so did Sergeant Charles Floyd until his sudden death near Sioux City, Iowa. His unfortunate loss and burial on a hill added two names to Clark's journal and map: Floyd's River and Floyd's Bluff.

The principal task of these journal-keepers, where place-names were concerned, was to match the known names on the Mackay and other maps, or in the minds of their French boatmen, with the geographic features they identified. A principal exception was the occasional creek, bluff, or island somehow identified with their own journey, as in the case of Floyd's death. When they counciled with the Indians above the mouth of the Platte, on a prominence near present Omaha, they called it Council Bluff. Historians ever after have been explaining that it is not the same as the later city of Council Bluffs, Iowa, on the eastern shore. When Private George Shannon became lost, and was an object of great concern, Shannon Creek was born and is now Ball Creek, in South Dakota. Trivialities begat names. Butter Island was christened when the expedition used the last of its butter, and No Preserves Island, above the mouth of the Niobrara, marked another depletion of the larder. Clark even gave one stream a name that he dreamed. In *The Field Notes of Captain William Clark* (New Haven, 1964), p. 112, Clark writes: "This Creek I call Roloje a name given me last night in my sleep." It is now Aowa Creek in Nebraska. His editor, Ernest S. Osgood, notes that the explorers already were "hard put to think up names."

A detailed study of the expedition's place-naming from St. Louis to the winter camp of 1804–5 awaits the travail of another student. In this essay we are moving ahead to even more promising ground, embracing mainly the present state of Montana, after we have seen how Lewis and Clark spent their winter among the Mandans and Hidatsas.

Confronting the Nameless Plains

Near two Mandan and three Hidatsa villages below the mouth of the Knife River, in present North Dakota, the Lewis and Clark Expedition built its winter quarters in the fall of 1804. It was to be called Fort Mandan.

As the Indian villages were a kind of regional trade center, other tribes were usually represented there; so were white traders from St. Louis or—much more frequently—from the Canadian trading houses to the north. The Hidatsas knew the western region as far as the Bitterroots, because they were raiders. They had traveled as far as the country of the Flatheads in the Bitterroot Valley, near the Continental Divide.

Considering the geographical knowledge of the Indians, and of men like Hugh Heney, Antoine Larocque, Charles McKenzie, and Hugh McCracken, who visited from the North West Company post on the Assiniboine, Fort Mandan was to become a kind of think tank (to utter a gross anachronism) for Lewis and Clark. Putting it another way, it became an extension of Jefferson's library in Virginia, where the President had helped Lewis plan the expedition. Here, before another fireside, as the northern snows grew deeper, the two explorers assembled and analyzed what they were being told by their white guests and by chiefs

Present State of Montana

such as Sheheke and Black Cat of the Mandans, and principal men of the Hidatsas.

When the ice began to leave the Missouri in early April, Lewis and Clark were ready to order their cumbersome keelboat back to St. Louis with a cargo of maps and other data, artifacts, and even a few living specimens of bird and animal life. Their plan was to "proceed on," a favorite term of Clark's, in two large pirogues and six smaller boats. The complement of soldiers had been trimmed down, but now they were accompanied by French interpreter Toussaint Charbonneau, his teenaged wife Sacagawea, and their infant son Jean Baptiste.

If we are to understand the naming problems facing the exploring team on the High Plains of Montana, and to prepare ourselves to observe the process by which these names were treated by succeeding generations, we must have a brief look at the nature of the material we have received from the hands of Lewis and Clark:

1. Notes made in the field. These rough drafts consisted of cartographic sketches, briefly noted observations, tables of course and distance, astronomical readings. Most scholars assume that such documents were accumulated throughout the expedition, but carelessly treated and mostly lost after they had been rendered into more permanent form. A notable exception is the sheaf of field notes which Clark made at the Wood River camp and on the journey to the Mandans, referred to above and commonly called the Osgood edition.

2. Revised manuscript materials, including daily journal entries written chronologically in bound notebooks and showing obvious signs of organization, reworking, and sometimes second-guessing. These include a large map made by Clark at Fort Mandan and sent downriver to Jefferson, in which all cartographic features beyond the Mandans are conjectural and secondhand; a similar map made at the completion of the expedition and dated 1806, representing the entire route plus information compiled from other sources; a large map in four sections, done by Clark in 1810 and intended to become engraver's copy for a published version; and several notebooks bound in red morocco, elkskin, or other coverings, which represented the most refined state of the explorers' observations that we have. Most of the material in this category did not become available to the public until late in the nineteenth century; some had been in private hands, and the red morocco notebooks had been stored away in the vaults of the American Philosophical Society in Philadelphia. The journals and most maps were edited by Reuben Gold

Thwaites and published as *Original Journals of the Lewis and Clark Expedition* (New York, 1904–5). A new edition is in preparation, edited by Gary E. Moulton and jointly sponsored by the American Philosophical Society and the Center for Great Plains Studies, University of Nebraska.

3. The only authorized publication of Lewis and Clark available to the public during most of the nineteenth century was *History of the Expedition under the Command of Captains Lewis and Clark* (Philadelphia, 1814; London, 1815 etc.). Although the title page states that it was "prepared for the press" by Paul Allen, the actual narrative was compiled and written by Philadelphia litterateur Nicholas Biddle. He had access to most of the journals including that of Sergeant Ordway, and received other information through correspondence and interviews with Clark and Private George Shannon (Lewis having died in 1809).

Except for some minor periodical publications, and Gass's weak edition of 1807, this was the scanty fare offered a nation of land-hungry and westward-looking Americans for decades. A wretchedly abstracted and distorted revision was published by Archibald McVickar in 1842, at the very time when the westward movement was gaining force. Finally, an edition carefully edited by Elliott Coues appeared in 1893.

If we are to know the Lewis and Clark names as the nineteenth-century public knew them, we must observe them solely as they appear in the Biddle edition. The manuscript journals are of course at our disposal for additional analysis.

Characteristics of Lewis and Clark Names

Busy and enthusiastic students of place-names, like the late George R. Stewart, who gave us *Names on the Land* (1945) and *American Place-Names* (1970) are forever classifying and reclassifying such names, the way botanists classify plants and for the same reason. It is an excellent way to get hold of the subject. Stewart, in his schedules of classification, proposed various ways of arranging place-names for study:

1. Descriptive names (Big Muddy Creek, let us say).
2. Associative names (The Pryor Mountains, through association with Pryor Creek).
3. Incident names (as in No Preserves Island, when the *confiture* ran out).
4. Possessive names (Werner's Creek).
5. Commemorative names (Fourth of July Creek).

6. Manufactured names (Roloje Creek, which Clark dreamed).

7. Shift names (if Lewis had named a place Locust Hill, after his Virginia birthplace).

The Lewis and Clark nomenclature is too simple to call for an elaborate classification scheme; we can manage with three categories. First are the places named for persons. The captains honored every member of the expedition with a place-name, some more than once. They honored their female friends, their President, and their dog. A second category is made up of occurrences. Did someone kill a grizzly bear today? Then let's call the nearest stream Yellow Bear Creek. But who killed the creature? Gibson did it, and a risky business it was. So let's call the stream Gibson's Creek instead, as he instigated an occurrence. A third category, by far the most frequently used, is derived from characteristics of the place named: Onion Island because of *Allium* plants found there, Ibex River from the prevalence of the bighorn sheep, Pine Island, Snow Mountains, Porcupine River.

We find none of Stewart's shift names, the favorites of westering pioneers during the time when Hillsdale, Iowa, might be named after someone's hometown of Hillsdale, Michigan, or a place christened New Salem to commemorate the old Salem so far back east.

It is almost as if Lewis and Clark were relying upon word association. An Indian sticklodge is found beside a stream; no need to rack one's mind for any name other than Sticklodge.

Because we do not know how the explorers kept their records, we must guess about how and when their place-names were contrived. There are enough examples in the Montana list to dispel the assumption that topographical features were always named when first encountered. It is safe to say that most names were given when sketch maps, journals, or tables of course and distance were being worked on around an evening campfire, or on a day when no travel was occurring, as when Lewis and Clark had to observe the sun from the same spot in midmorning and midafternoon for a latitude reading. The journals and maps are filled with signs of interlining, erasing, and other evidence of second thoughts. Sergeant Ordway's journal, apparently unrevised after the entries were written, mentions the naming of Werner's River—in the Montana area—but not those streams named for Sacagawea, Thompson, Shields, Pryor, Whitehouse, Frazer, or himself.

We see this delayed naming in the records kept by Clark when he brought a separate party down the Yellowstone on the homeward journey.

His passage was so rapid, about sixty miles a day, that he was to leave the names of Yellowstone tributaries in disarray, even though he usually got the lines drawn properly on his maps.

There are good reasons why the naming in Montana was difficult. The terrain was uninspiring in the eastern part, where the temptation to name every waterless rivulet Little Dry Creek must have been strong. Also, there were no informants at hand, either French or Indian, who had seen this area. The Mandans and Hidatsas had named the larger rivers for the explorers, but there was no one to call upon for the smaller ones. Until Lewis and Clark reached the Shoshonis near the present Idaho border they saw no Indians, although they encountered many signs of their presence. This lack of contact is a singular coincidence, as the area was the home or hunting grounds of the Assiniboins, Blackfeet, Crows, Crees, Salish, Kalispels, Kutenais, and Shoshonis.

The Indian names passed on in translation by Lewis and Clark are robust and solid names: the Big Horn, the Musselshell, Beaverhead Valley, Great Falls, Shishequaw Mountain. The captains produced some memorable ones of their own, too—the Madison, Jefferson, and Gallatin; Judith's River; Gates of the Mountains—but their weak names are more prevalent. Prince Maximilian of Wied, traveling by keelboat on the Upper Missouri in 1833, was amused to encounter Teapot Creek in the Biddle edition. "We could not help observing that such names are not well chosen, especially as it would not be difficult to find better ones, even by retaining the generally harmonious Indian names" (Maximilian, 23:61). It was an easy observation for the educated and traveled prince to make, especially as he was accompanied by Indian, French, and American fur-trading employees who knew the country. His comment does, however, offer one reason why so few Lewis and Clark names survived. They deserved no better fate.

The Winds of Change

There is more than one way of looking at the processes of place-naming and changes in names. A conventional view is that the person who names a place has a kind of perpetual right to expect retention of the name. Surveyor W. W. De Lacy wrote in 1876 of a "general rule governing geographers," authorizing the discoverer of a geographic feature to name it for himself or give it any name he liked (Wheat, 3:153). Elliott Coues felt strongly about this where Lewis and Clark names were involved, and so did O. D. Wheeler, his contemporary, who accused the government and the nation's scientific societies of ignoring the "rightness" of the Lewis and Clark names (Wheeler, 2:50).

An opposite view holds that the assignment of any place-name is basically a re-naming process, for other peoples, in earlier and unrecorded times, may have had their own names for the same places. Thus it is not a cultural trespass but rather a cultural change, when old names disappear and new ones are coined; even deliberate and knowing change is legitimate. In any case, this view holds, it is no more possible to slow or halt the coming and going of place-names than it is to regulate the ebb and flow of language over centuries or even decades. A place-name will change if the present generation dislikes or is ignorant of an earlier name, or simply prefers one of its own.

It might be said that the erosion of Lewis and Clark names began the day they were published by the firm of Bradford and Inskeep, of Philadelphia, in 1814. The company was in deep financial trouble and would produce only one printing of the book (William Clark did not see a copy until March 1816). Although there were English and European editions, the total distribution could not have been large.

Cartographers, eager to add new data to their own maps of the West, made immediate use of the Biddle edition. Borrowings from the Biddle map, with all its distortions and omissions, began to appear in commercial maps immediately. This may have looked like progress to men and women with an eye to westward development, but actually there was no pressing need for the Biddle information; no one was yet out there to use it.

By the 1840s, when America was at last ready for the Oregon and California trails, the Gold Rush, and steamboat travel to inland waters, few copies of the original Biddle edition were available. A new version, edited by Archibald McVickar in 1842, was abridged, paraphrased, and its map distorted. We can never be sure which edition is meant when a diarist or historian of those days refers to "Lewis and Clarke." Explorer Jedediah Smith is described as considering the Lewis and Clark journals and map as a basic guidebook to a vast wilderness. Only the original version was available to him. But half a century later, pioneer Montanan James Stuart wrote: "Lewis and Clarke have played us out; if we had left the notes and map of their route at home and followed the Indian trail, we would have saved four days' travel." He is likely to have been carrying the McVickar edition.

The first class of westerners that actively ignored Lewis and Clark names was the fur traders. British traders from Canada already had their own names. Peter Skene Ogden, of the Hudson's Bay Company, considered Clark's River to be the Flathead during an 1825 trip into Mantana. To Alexander Ross, another Canadian, a stretch of Clark Fork was already the Bitterroot. Much further west (and not within the purview of our study), names given by the Astorians from the United States did not stick, either, for British influence was too strong. Tributaries of the Snake River in present Idaho and Washington were still known as the Malheur, Owyhee, Bruneau, Goose Creek, Raft River, Portneuf, &c. (Wheat, 2:76).

American fur traders from St. Louis continued to expand their hunting grounds in Montana, and to change Lewis and Clark names as well as create new ones. A tenable conjecture is that travelers in the West who made maps adopted Lewis and Clark names where they had not themselves traveled, adding their own names in areas they knew. An example is trader W. A. Ferris, whose map of the Northwest drawn in 1836 uses the 1814 Biddle edition extensively (even to the extent of copying an engraver's error in one case), but used the term Big Hole for the valley then known to trappers by that name, instead of Wisdom Valley. Eventually, with establishments such as Fort Union at the extreme eastern side of the Montana region, and the Missouri and Yellowstone rivers populated by posts such as Forts Alexander, Cass, McKenzie, Benton, Sarpy, and Van Buren, the area was peopled with semi-permanent residents who may or may not have had access to Lewis and Clark names, and whose constant contact with local topographical features gave them an opportunity to devise new place-names.

The next group of name-changers were the Jesuits, who came to western Montana in the 1840s. Although these men, notably Father Pierre De Smet, left some lasting names, their total impact was small. For a note on this period, see under Clark's River in the listing below.

By midcentury, all the talk was of railroads. Rails had revolutionized trade and commerce in the East and were inching toward the Mississippi, offering a threat to the steamboat trade. That one day the first track would be laid west of the Missouri and then on to the Pacific coast no one doubted. As part of the system, wagon roads would lead to the railheads. Wagon trains to Oregon, California, and points between already had marked out routes that would become future railroad lines and highways, but now the government must do in a professional way what the wagonmasters and wandering horsemen had done as trailbreakers.

Plans were drawn for four surveys to be made from the Midwest to the Pacific, as a means of deciding on the most practical and economical route. With the Army Corps of Topographical Engineers providing guidance, teams of surveyors and their support groups were formed into what was to be called the Pacific Railway Surveys. The survey of most interest to us in the present study is the northern one, extending from St. Paul, Minnesota, to Washington Territory, and directed by Isaac I. Stevens.

Stevens was a West Point engineer and veteran of the Mexican War, and at the age of thirty-five had been named governor of Washington Territory. Later he would serve as a general in the Civil War, dying in action in 1862. In the many splendid maps that resulted from Stevens's leadership, and from the support of men such as Lieutenant A. J. Donelson, Alexander Culbertson, Lieutenant John Mullan, Captain W. F. Raynolds, and a superior topographer, Lieutenant Gouveneur K. Warren, we see the coming of a new era. Mapmaking was no longer an amateur's game or a sideline, but a combination of art, craft, and science with a serious national purpose.

Basically, however, the procedures of the Stevens survey were no different from those of Lewis and Clark. The team gathered all the previous maps it could find, obtained the best instruments available and men to use them, and hired guides who knew the region being surveyed. The result, as can be seen from the listing of place-names from the Biddle edition and the dating of the changes that have occurred, is that the Stevens party was responsible for the disappearance of many Lewis and Clark names.

Let us imagine how Isaac Stevens himself might have explained it:

We had the Lewis and Clark material and respected it. But try conferring beside a stream, surrounded by men who have lived in the area all their lives, or at least traveled it thoroughly, and insisting that the stream should be mapped as Battle River because of an incident that happened in 1806. It is the 1850s now, and these men have always known the stream as Birch Creek. It is a traditional name. "And who," the grizzled old trappers might ask, "are Lewis and Clark? They only passed through. We've trapped these creeks, married into the tribes, wintered in these mountains all our lives. Where does it say we can't name our own places?" It is hard not to side with these men, especially when the names they have preserved are Indian names with a stronger claim to life than those of Lewis and Clark.

After the surveyors came the gold prospectors. When gold was found is a matter of dispute, but by 1862 the news of gold findings at Bannack, in western Montana, sent an alert to miners far and near. These men, and soon their women, came with crude maps or none at all, but with a special need for place-names to guide them to the site of the latest rumored strike. The first notable Lewis and Clark place-name to fall seems to have been Willard's Creek, changed to Grasshopper Creek.

Within three years, Washington Territory had been divided to create Montana Territory, and an official map was drawn by W. W. De Lacey for the new legislature. De Lacey had surveyed in person as well as studied extant maps, and his own cartographic work was a mixture of both efforts. Some of his place-names, especially in the eastern portion of the territory where settlement was sparse, were straight from the Biddle edition. But there were new names aplenty, not all of them topographic. Towns with names such as Silver Bow City, Gallatin City, Virginia, and Deer Lodge City had appeared. Other names would come out of necessity, and names for creeks, gulches, buttes, and valleys would be assigned by settlers with no inclination and perhaps no opportunity to decide whether Lewis and Clark had passed that way.

In 1872, a small group of Montanans set out to determine the feasibility of navigation by steamboats of light draft, running between Three Forks and Fort Benton. They were familiar with Lewis and Clark's names, and used them in referring to such major watercourses as the Madison, Gallatin, and Dearborn rivers. But for smaller streams, and points of interest along the way, they created new names freely. Traveling downriver from Three Forks, they produced such names as Eagle Rocks, Red Rock Canyon, Sixteenmile Creek, the Belt Range, Goose Rapids, Duck Creek, White Gulch, Confederate Creek, Black Crook Dens, and Bear's Tooth Mountain. At the foot of an island they called Milnor Island, where a great stone sugarloaf rose 800 feet beside the river, they named it North Pacific Rock (Roberts, 206–35). The day had arrived when every spring, rivulet, or projecting stone had to have a name; the day of the Lewis and Clark names was over. By the end of the nineteenth century it had become prudent to establish a national agency, the Board on Geographic Names, to monitor the naming of place to avoid confusion and duplication.

The explorers gave us, in the Biddle edition, 148 names in the area we now call Montana. Of these, 20 were Indian names either transliterated or translated, and half of them have survived. The names Lewis and Clark devised themselves have met a harsher fate. Of the 128 they left us, only 17 are in use today.

A dozen years after the two captains crossed the continent, Simon McGillivray of the British-controlled North West Company wrote a "Statement Relative to the Columbia River and Adjoining Territory." He complained that the boundaries of the Louisiana Purchase were ill defined, and that the United States took full advantage of this fact in drawing the boundaries "as extensive and undefined as possible." He continued:

> With a view therefore, to extend their territorial claims across the Continent to the Pacifick Ocean, and to establish a communication therewith through the rivers Missouri and Columbia, the American government in the year 1806 [1804] fitted out an expedition to explore the Country under the command of Captains Lewis and Clarke, who proceeded to the head of the river Missouri, thence across the Rocky Mountains to the river Columbia, and so down to the mouth of that river, from whence they returned by the same route.
>
> In order to give this Expedition as much as possible the air of a voyage of discovery, and to make it appear as if they were exploring and taking possession of an unknown Country (tho' in fact the Country in the Interior was well known to the traders from Canada) the Americans, as they went along, bestowed new names on Rivers, Mountains, i.e. such as Jefferson's River, Madison's River and so forth, forgetting or affecting to forget that the Columbia River had already been surveyed by Captain [George] Vancouver, and that a route across the Continent to the Pacifick Ocean had already been traversed by Sir Alexander McKenzie, both of whom as well as Captain [James] Cook, had taken possession of the Country in the name of His Majesty as herein before mentioned [15 November 1817, FO 5/123/ 187-88, Public Record Office, London].

If there is a moral or bromide here, it is that naming places does not make them yours, especially in geopolitical matters. You must negotiate, maneuver, or go to war for them. As a corollary, the naming of places is not an act of permanence. Give the name Jefferson River to a stream and it may chance to live for centuries. Give the name Martha's River to another stream and it may have become the Big Muddy before the name-giver has lived out his years. It is the flux, the fragility, the role of happenstance, and the waywardness of human nature in the handing down of place-names that make their study so worthy a subject.

Montana: A Case Study

All abbreviations, except YS for Yellowstone River, MR for Missouri River, MRC for Missouri River Commission, and GLO for General Land Office, are self-explanatory. Minor variants in place-names (creek, river, fork, branch) are ignored in presenting earlier terminology unless the variants are significant.

Names in boldface are spelled as they appear in the Biddle edition as edited by Coues or in its accompanying map. The first paragraph (A) lists the present name as found in publications of the U.S. Geological Survey. The second paragraph (B) lists earlier names, followed by sources (such as Warren, 1857), that represent the authors of maps or other publications in the list of references. The third and following paragraphs, if present, consist of discussion and miscellaneous information.

A glance at the dates of references in paragraph B provides a guide to the period in which the original Lewis and Clark name fell into disuse. The absence of paragraph B for many names indicates lack of recorded information, especially for minor topographic features.

APSAHSOOHA RIVER

A. Rock Creek, joining Clarks Fork of the YS from w. in Carbon Co.

B. Apsahsooha River (Tanner, 1822); Absarooke Fork (Ferris, 1836); Rocky Fork (Russell, 1834–43).

Clark did not see this stream while descending the Yellowstone, and the name is not in the Biddle text nor in either Clark's journal or his field map. It appears on Clark's 1810 manuscript map as Apsarooka Fork, and misspelled on the printed Biddle map of 1814. The source is George Drouillard, the expedition's interpreter whose later travels in the Yellowstone country were recounted to Lewis and Clark in 1808. A map produced by Clark and annotated by both Clark and Lewis from Drouillard's data is in the Missouri Historical Society and reproduced in Skarsten (1964). This map shows the Apsarooka as a branch of Clarks Fork, with the notation that a band of Crows always wintered there because of a kind of grass which they liked for their horses. The note is in Lewis's hand, dated 6 Sept. 1808.

Variants of the name Absaroka are now generally applied to the entire Crow tribe.

ARGALIA CREEK

A. Smith Creek, entering the YS from e. in Richland Co.

B. Argalia River (Burr, 1839; Warren, 1855; De Lacy, 1865).

Together with the grizzly bear, the pronghorn, and the mountain goat, the now-familiar bighorn or mountain sheep was an object of fascination to the men of the expedition. The problem they had in deciding what to call the animal is revealed in the variety of streams they named for it. The present listing contains Argalia Creek, Argalia River, Big Horn River, Little Big Horn River, Ibex Creek, Ibex Island, and Ibex River.

To zoologists, the argali is an Asian member of the *Capra* or goat genus, and the ibex belongs to the *Ovis* or sheep genus. Both have large, recurved horns, and it made sense for Lewis and Clark, and the scientists who reviewed their specimens, to consider the bighorn as being related to one or the other of these Asian species.

In the fall of 1804, when the expedition was among the Teton Sioux in present South Dakota, Clark wrote in his journal (1:169) that he had seen a spoon made of "a horn of an anemele of the sheep kind." Later he interlined the words "mountain ram of Argalia." The men were to see no live bighorns until the following spring, but were able to send back to Jefferson, as they were leaving their wintering grounds at the Mandan villages, "4 horns of the mountain ram, or *big horn*" (Jackson, 1:235). In reporting on these to the French savant C. F. C. Volney, Jefferson wrote that the horns were "perhaps a species of the *Ovis Ammon*" (Jackson, 1:291). This name had been assigned the ibex by scientists, and today the bighorn is classified as a related species, *Ovis canadensis.*

Despite the background that Lewis, and to a much lesser extent Clark, possessed in natural history, neither was likely to arrive at the words argali or ibex unaided. Among the books we know the captains were carrying was an edition of Linnaeus, the founder of the current system of Latin classification, and from whom the name "argali" may have come. Also in the expedition's little library was a four-volume set, *A New and Complete Dictionary of the Arts and Sciences,* second edition, 1764, possibly on loan from Jefferson's library. A drawing of the ibex appears in plate CXLII of the dictionary — actually an encyclopedia — and on p. 1718 is the description: "an animal of the goat kind, with extremely long, nodose horns, which bend backwards, and are of a blackish colour, and annular on the surface." This engraving and description are reflected in the statement by Sergeant Gass that Captain Clark "says they resemble that animal more than any other."

The first indication that Clark had been thumbing through what he called his "Deckinsery of arts an ciences" appears in his journal entry of 25 May 1805 (2:75), when he reports seeing "a female *Ibi* or big horn animal." The captains began to use ibex and argali interchangeably from then on, eventually settling on the terms mountain sheep and bighorn as the names with which they felt most comfortable.

The creek encountered by Clark near the end of his Yellowstone exploration is Argalia Creek on his 1810 manuscript map and the Biddle map, but Ibex River in the Biddle text (3:1166). The stream appears as Ibex Creek on the Maximilian version of Clark's field map — the only copy surviving — drawn some time after the expedition. Clark's journal notes the presence of bighorns in the vicinity of the stream.

ARGALIA RIVER [OR CREEK]

    A. Wolf Creek, entering the MR from n. in Roosevelt Co.

    B. Fort Charles River (Holmes Expedition of 1864 in White, 128).

Not in the Biddle text nor in any of the journals, and not charted on Clark's field map, but shown on his 1810 map as Argalia C. or R. (the paper is worn), and on the Biddle map. The name apparently was seleced after the original journals and maps were completed, as the original name in the journals is Lackwater Creek. There is nothing in the journals to suggest the sighting of bighorn sheep in the area.

ASH RAPIDS

    A. Drowned Mans Rapids between Chouteau and Fergus cos., at mi. 749 (MRC map of 1892–95, sheet 73).

    The Biddle text (1:334) reads: "Near this spot are a few trees of the ash, the first we have seen for a great distance, and from which we named the place Ash Rapids."

BAPTIST CREEK

    A. Pompeys Pillar Creek, entering the YS from n. in Yellowstone Co.

    B. Baptist Creek (Ferris, 1836; Warren, 1855).

This name was originally applied to a stream entering the YS from the s., which was then renamed Shannons River. It is surprising that Clark waited until the homeward leg of the journey to name two geographical features after Sacagawea's infant son, Jean Baptiste. This creek is named on his 1810 map and the printed Biddle map. Clark's manuscript journal notes a stream opposite Pompey's Pillar (see below) as "a large Brook on the Lar[boar]d Side I call baptiests creek." Very fond of the youngster, Clark called him Pomp or Pompy, and later played a role in the boy's education in St. Louis.

BARN MOUNTAIN

    A. Highwood Baldy of the Highwood Mts. in s. Chouteau Co.

    B. West or Belt Butte (Coues, 1893).

    Biddle (1:347) says this mountain was so named "from its resemblance to the roof of a barn." Later usage converted it to a butte.

BATTLE RIVER

    A. Birch Creek, entering the Marias R. from w. in Pondera Co.

    B. Battle River (Tanner, 1822; Ferris, 1836; Burr, 1839); Birch Creek (Stevens, 1855; Raynolds, 1868; De Lacy, 1865).

On the return route of the expedition, the party split into three groups: Clark to explore the Yellowstone to its mouth, Ordway to take a few men directly to the old campsites at Great Falls, and Lewis to take a more northerly track which would include an inspection of the Marias in the hope that the river would extend the boundaries of the Louisiana Purchase farther north than then believed. Disappointed in this belief—he named his northernmost campsite Camp Disappointment—Lewis and his party turned back toward the Missouri. On the south side of Two Medicine River, an affluent of the Marias southwest of the town of Cut Bank, Lewis and his men fought an engagement with a small band of Piegans. When some of the Indians attempted to steal horses, the ensuing skirmish resulted in the killing of at least two Indians.

The stream Clark calls Battle River on his 1810 manuscript map and the Biddle map is not Two Medicine River, the site of the episode, but another affluent several miles to the south.

BEAR RAPID
A. Bear Rapids, above Custer Creek in Prairie Co.
B. Shown on some early maps including Warren, 1857.

BEAVER RIVER
A. Lower Deer Creek, entering the YS from s. in Sweet Grass Co.
B. Beaver Fork (Ferris, 1836); Beaver or Big Rock Creek (Raynolds, 1868).

On 17 July 1806, the same day he notes the two "Rivers-Across," he observed two creeks downstream that very nearly qualified as cross creeks: Beaver River from the s. and Otter River from the n. On his manuscript, both these names have been written over erasures.

BEAVERHEAD VALLEY
A. Valley of the Beaverhead R. extending e. to South Boulder Creek on the YS.

BEAVER'S HEAD
A. Beaverhead, a rocky prominence at the e. edge of Beaverhead Co. line, about 12 mi. s.w. of Twin Bridges, and at one time locally confused with Rattlesnake Cliffs.
B. Same (Ferris, 1836, and later maps).

BIGDRY RIVER

A. Still the Big Dry, and now a large southern arm of Fort Peck Reservoir in McCone Co. Lewis called it "the bed of the most extraordinary river that I ever beheld," being half a mile wide and completely dry.

BIG DRY RIVER

A. Sunday Creek, entering the YS from s.w. in Custer Co.

This stream was used as a boundary designator in an 1851 treaty with the Assiniboin, Blackfeet, and Crow tribes (Kappler, 2:595), but mistakenly described as entering the YS opposite the Powder River. The name appears on Clark's field map (O'Fallon tracing), his 1810 manuscript map, and the printed Biddle version.

BIGHORN RIVER

A. Bighorn River, entering the YS from s. in Treasure Co.

B. Big Horn River (Burr, 1839; Raynolds, 1868; Warren, 1857; Stuart, 1863); Horn (Larpenteur, 1899).

The captains learned of the Bighorn by its Mandan name, Arsata with variant spellings, before leaving the Mandan villages. As they did not hesitate to give the same name to affluents of larger and distinct river courses, they soon affixed the name temporarily to an affluent of the Missouri (see immediately below). When Clark was descending the Yellowstone and keeping an eye out for the Bighorn of today, he at first assigned the name to the wrong stream—Clarks Fork—but eventually got it straightened out on his field map. It appears on the Biddle map, but the engraver has labeled only the branch called Little Big Horn, leaving the larger stream unlabeled.

Biddle wrote: "This is the river which has been described by the Indians as rising in the Rocky Mountains, near the Yellowstone and the sources of the Platte, and then finding its way through the Cote Noir [Black Hills] and the eastern range of the Rocky Mountains" (3:1153). The concept of the Black Hills was not nearly so constricted then as is the isolated mountainous area in South Dakota which we know as the Black Hills today.

BIG HORN RIVER

Clark's first choice of names for the Judith R., and mistakenly engraved on his 1814 map upriver from the Judith.

BIRTH CREEK
A. Whitetail Creek, entering the Jefferson R. from n. in Jefferson Co. It can be said that Lewis and Clark were occasionally tone deaf as they assigned place-names. The name Birthday Creek, in honor of Clark's birthday on 1 Aug. 1805, might have stuck in the minds of the American people. But Birth Creek is too vague.

BLOWINGFLY CREEK
A. Squaw Creek, entering the MR from e. in Garfield Co. below the mouth of the Musselshell.

BRATTON'S RIVER
A. Bridger Creek, entering the YS from s. in Sweet Grass Co. On the map only.
B. Bratten Fork (Ferris, 1836).

BRATTON'S RIVER
A. Timber Creek, entering the MR from n. in Valley Co. Listed in Clark's summary statement only.
B. Bratton's River (Tanner, 1822; Ferris, 1836); Timber Creek (Raynolds, 1868).
First called Rattlesnake Creek in the journals.

BROKEN MOUNTAINS
A. Sweet Grass Hills, near the Canadian border in Toole Co.
B. Same in Stevens, 1855.

BROWN BEAR-DEFEATED CREEK
A. Snow Creek, entering Fort Peck Reservoir from s. in Garfield Co.
The naming of this stream reveals not only the problems that Lewis and Clark had in naming places appropriately, but in particular the perplexing question of whether the grizzly bear was brown, yellow, white, or grizzled. Two incidents involving grizzlies are recorded on the same sheet of Clark's field maps, 20 (Moulton, pl. 50). On 13 May 1805 Gibson wounded a "brown bear" but did not pursue him. Hence Gibson's Creek, below. An episode involving six men occurred on 14 May. Clark's journal entry of 17 May speaks of the slain bear as "brown or yellow." In their summation of courses and distances, Lewis called the stream "Brown bear defeat," while Clark chose "Yellow bear defeat." Clark already had

named the stream Rose Creek, but he struck this and wrote Yellow Bear Defeat Creek, later changing yellow to brown. But there were more changes to come. On the 1810 map that he prepared for his publisher, Clark called the stream White Bear Creek—and the engraver misread it Whitebeard Creek, as it appears in the published map.

BUFFALO CREEK

A. Pondera Coulee, entering the Marias R. from w. in Liberty Co.

B. Buffalo River (Burr, 1839); Antelope Creek (Coues, 1893); Pondera Creek (White, 1966).

Pondera is a corruption of Pend d'Oreilles, an Indian tribe named for their earrings.

BUFFALOE SHOALS

A. Buffalo Rapids from the mouth of Sunday Creek, entering the YS from w. in Custer Co. and extending about 6 mi. downstream (Raynolds, 1868).

BULL CREEK

A. Dog Creek, entering the MR from s. in Fergus Co., just below the mouth of the Judith.

B. Bull Creek (Tanner, 1822); Dog Creek (Stevens, 1855).

Named "from the circumstance of a Buffalow Bull swiming from the opposit side and comeing out of the river . . . and passing with great violence thro' our camp in the night . . . without hurting a man, altho' they lay in every direction, and it was very dark" (Clark, 28 May 1805, in Thwaites, 2:90).

BURNTLODGE CREEK

A. Seven Blackfoot Creek, entering the MR from s. in Garfield Co.

B. Burntlodge Creek (Tanner, 1822; Ferris, 1836); Quarrel Creek (Raynolds, 1868).

An example of two names being given to the same geographic feature because the party did not always travel together and have the same experiences. Lewis called this stream Rattlesnake Creek because Clark was nearly bitten by a snake there (1:312). But Clark called it Burnt Lodge Creek because of a fire that occurred in their skin lodge. Clark's version prevailed, and appears in Moulton, pl. 50.

CAMP DISAPPOINTMENT

A. On the s. bank of Cut Bank Creek, about 12 mi. n.e. of Browning in Glacier Co.

The name Lewis gave to the camp near the Marias when he decided the course of that river was not going to extend the northern boundary of the Louisiana Purchase as he had hoped. He may have intended it as a pun on Cape Disappointment, on the Pacific coast.

CLARK'S FORK

A. Entering the YS from s. in Yellowstone Co.

B. Same on all maps inspected.

When he first encountered this stream, Clark thought it might be the Big Horn, of which he had been told by the Indians at Fort Mandan. He so named it, but later, upon discovering the actual Big Horn, he renamed this stream Clark's Fork. The name is one of the few surviving names of expedition members in Montana.

CLARK'S RIVER

A. Also called Clark Fork, a branch of the Columbia originating in western Montana.

A part of the Columbia River system, this river of about 325 mi. originates in southwest Montana near Butte. It flows northward to Deer Lodge and northwest to Missoula, then to Pend Oreille Lake in Idaho. The stream is generally called the Pend Oreille from this point on, as it leaves the lake and flows toward the Columbia, although Lewis and Clark recognized it as part of the Clark system. They were familiar with two of its major tributaries, the Bitterroot (which they called the west fork of Clark's River) and the Blackfoot (which they called the River of the Road to the Buffalo). They did not see a third major affluent, the Flathead, which comes south and joins the main river near Paradise, Montana, but there is evidence in the maps and journals that they at first referred to Clark's Fork as the Flathead, obtaining the name from Indian sources. In fact, it may be that they did not apply the name Clark's Fork to what is now the Bitterroot-Clark-Pend Oreille system until sometime during the return journey. Moulton concludes that the name was assigned between 17 April and 6 May 1806 (see Moulton, pp. 10–11, and pls. 95, 97, 102).

Clark Fork began to lose its identity early, as trappers, miners, and surveyors named its tributaries and renamed sections of the main river. By 1836, Warren Ferris was calling the upper branches the Bitterroot and the Blackfoot. Father Pierre De Smet, upon establishing St. Mary's Mission in the Bitterroot Valley in the early 1840s, applied the name St. Mary's to the river, the mountain near it, the mission itself, and the valley. He named another reach of the river the St. Regis de Borgia, but shifted that name to a tributary, the present St. Regis River (Thwaites, 27:335). The maps published by De Smet contain a few "catholicized" names, but an unpublished manuscript map now in the archives of St. Louis University is an ecclesiastical map in which every affluent of the Clark and other major rivers is given the name of a saint or a religious connotation.

In 1855, surveyor Isaac I. Stevens considered Clark Fork to be formed by the junction of the Flathead system from the north and the Bitterroot system from the south, joining "opposite Horse Plain." Other names soon were applied to parts of the system. A gold-rush diarist of the 1860s wrote: "We camp near . . . which the Bitter-root river joins with the Hell-gate river, & forms what is called the St. Mary's, Hell-Gate, or Missoula River" (White, 67n).

In an effort to clarify the nomenclature, the U.S. Board on Geographic Names (4th Report, 1890–1916, p. 70) declared Clark Fork to be "Not Bitter Root, Bitterroot, Clarke, Clarks River, Deer Lodge, Hell Gate, Hellgate, Missoula, Silver Bow, nor Silverbow." U.S. Geological Survey maps of today conform to Stevens's description of 1855 — the Bitterroot and Flathead systems joining to form the main watercourse called Clark Fork.

B.   Same on all maps inspected.

COAL RIVER

A.   O'Fallon Creek, entering the YS from s.e. in Prairie Co.

B.   Oaktaroup River, the Indian name (De Lacy, 1865).

The present name commemorates Benjamin O'Fallon, Clark's nephew, who operated in the area as an associate of the American Fur Company. Clark recorded the name of this river at Fort Mandan under the names Arktarha or Oketarpassahha, and by the time it appeared in the Biddle edition it had become Oaktaroup.

COKALAHISHKIT. SEE RIVER OF THE ROAD TO THE BUFFALO.

CREVICE CREEK

A.   Perhaps the stream entering the MR from s. at a place called Hole in the Wall (MRC map of 1892–95, sheet 74).

CROOKED FALLS
A. One of the falls at Great Falls, named by the explorers. See under Great Falls.

DEARBORN'S RIVER
A. Dearborn River, entering the MR from n. in Lewis Co.
B. Unchanged on all maps, except for occasional use of possessive.
By mid-July 1805, the explorers were getting into country where the names assigned would carry greater prestige back home and it was necessary to put a little order into the process. They already had named a lesser stream for Secretary of the Navy Robert Smith (see Smith's River), who had played but a small role in the sponsorship of the expedition. Now, three days later, they had come to a stream nearly as large as the Missouri itself. Lewis wrote: "This handsome bold and clear stream we name in honour of the Secretary of war calling it Dearborn's river" (Thwaites, 2:243–44). Still to come were rivers to be named for Thomas Jefferson, James Madison, and Albert Gallatin.
The name appears to have been given by Lewis acting alone. He was keeping the day's record on 18 July 1805, including course and distance, while Clark was out scouting for signs of friendly Indians. The name Dearborn's River appears twice in Lewis's entry, including the course and distance record. In Clark's briefer entry, the phrase "we call Dearbourne's river after the Sety. of War" appears to have been inserted.
For a brief time the Dearborn carried the name Torrent, when Lewis failed to recognize it during his side trip on the homeward journey. It appears as Torrent in Gass's journal, and as Torrant (changed to Dearborne's) in Lewis's journal.

DRY CREEK
A. White Beaver Creek, entering the YS from n. in Stillwater Co.
B. Dry Creek (Ferris, 1836).

ELK CREEK
Alkali Creek, entering the YS from n. in Treasure Co.

ELK RAPIDS
A. One of a series of rapids below the Judith, along the southern boundary of Blaine Co.
B. Elk Rapids (Ferris, 1836).
Ordway (219) called this place "Elk & faun riffle," riffle being a

common term for rapids. "We saw a dow Elk & faun" there, he wrote. In modern times, Stearns has identified the place as Bird Rapids, the campsite for 26 May 1805.

FIELD'S CREEK

A. Charbonneau Creek, entering the YS from e. in McKenzie Co., N.D.

"Jo: Fields River" on the extant copy of a sketch Clark made of Yellowstone tributaries, from Indian sources, while he was still at the Mandan villages in 1804–5. Thus it must have been added later, after Pvt. Joseph Field was sent several miles up the Yellowstone and "discovered a large creek falling into the Yellowstone River on the S.E. Side 8 miles up near which he saw a big horned animal" (Thwaites, 1:343).

FIELDS' CREEK

A. Boulder River, entering the MR from n. in Jefferson Co.

FLATTERY RUN

A. Sand Coulee, entering the Great Falls area from s.

Clark appears to have called this stream a "flattery run" because it gave the appearance of being longer than it was, containing only about a mile of water from its mouth (see Thwaites 2:173 and 6:8). The term is not in the Oxford English Dictionary (see Criswell, 1940).

FLOWER CREEK

A. Warm Springs Creek, flowing into the Bitterroot R. from s.w. in Ravalli Co. near Ross Hole. Lewis and Clark called it Flour Camp Creek when they ran out of flour here.

FORT CREEK

A. Horse Creek, entering the YS from n. about opposite the Rosebud R. in Rosebud Co.

B. Fort Creek (Ferris, 1836).

"In one of the low bottoms of the river was an Indian fort, which seemed to have been built last summer," Biddle wrote (3:1140). The creek is shown only on the map.

FORT MOUNTAIN

A. Square Butte in n.w. Cascade Co.

FORT MOUNTAIN CREEK
A. Little Muddy Creek, entering the MR from n. in Cascade Co.
B. Fort Mountain or Muddy Creek (MRC map of 1892–95, sheet 78).

FRAZIER'S CREEK
A. South Boulder River, entering the Jefferson R. from s. in Madison Co.
Named for Pvt. Robert Frazer, a member of the expedition.

FRAZIER'S RAPIDS
A. See entry above. Coues (2:454) calls them South Boulder Rapids.

GALLATIN'S RIVER
A. Gallatin River, entering the MR from s.e. in Gallatin Co. as part of the Three Forks. See under Three Forks.

GASS' CREEK
A. Crow Creek, entering the MR from n. in Broadwater Co.
B. Hot or Warm Springs Creek (Coues, 1893).
Named for Sgt. Patrick Gass, elected sergeant upon the death of Charles Floyd, and one of the six enlisted men probably keeping journals. The journals of four of the men have survived, in whole or part, and the Gass journal was the first to be published. Its appearance in 1807 preceded the Biddle narrative and map of 1814.

GATES OF THE ROCKY MOUNTAINS
A. In Lewis and Clark Co., at the n.w. tip of Helena National Forest. Always so called, but often "Gate of the Mountains," this term may have been suggested by descriptions provided by the Mandans, although the name itself was devised by Lewis.

GIBSON'S CREEK
A. Sutherland Creek, entering Fort Peck Reservoir from n. in Valley Co.
B. Gibson's Creek (Tanner, 1822; Ferris, 1836; Burr, 1839; De Lacy, 1865).
Named for Pvt. George Gibson, a member of the expedition who had an encounter with a grizzly near this place.

GIBSON'S RIVER

A. Glendive Creek, entering the YS from s. in Dawson Co.

B. Gibson's River (Warren, 1855); Glendive's Creek (Stanley, 1874). The name is interlined in Clark's journal as if added later.

GLADE CREEK

A. Affluent of North Fork Creek, entering the Big Hole R. from w. in Beaverhead Co.

GOODRICH'S ISLAND

A. Coues (1326) thought this island had disappeared by 1893.

GREAT FALLS OF THE MISSOURI

A. Still so named, at the city of Great Falls, Cascade Co.

Several of the names now attached to various features of the falls were not assigned by Lewis and Clark. They referred to the largest cascade as Great Falls, and used the term to indicate the entire area. But they also used such terms as sulphur spring, beautiful cascade, and large fountain, with no suggestion that these were anything more than descriptive terms. Crooked Falls is not shown on Clark's sketch (Thwaites, 2:176), and Colter's Falls—no longer visible—was applied by later travelers. The name Great Falls came from the Indians at Fort Mandan.

GROG SPRING

Neither Coues in 1893 nor Wheeler in 1905 could find this spring below Great Falls, where Clark refreshed his men with a ration of whisky in the summer of 1805. It was located at Cracon-du-Nez, a narrow strip of land where the Teton River edges to within a hundred yards of the Missouri.

GROUSE CREEK

A. Beauchamp Creek, entering the MR from n. in Chouteau Co.

B. Beauchamp Creek (Stevens, 1855).

Named after the sighting of a flock of sharp-tailed grouse in the area.

GULF IN THE ISLAND BEND

A. About 8 mi. below the mouth of the Milk R.

The word "gulf" is here used in the sense of a whirlpool (Criswell, 1940).

HOTSPRING VALLEY
A. Big Hole Valley in Beaverhead and Deer Lodge cos.
B. Big Hole Prairie (Raynolds, 1868; Warren, 1857).

HOWARD'S CREEK
A. Sixteenmile Creek, entering the MR from e. in Broadwater Co.
B. Green Creek (Coues, 1893).
Named for Pvt. Thomas P. Howard, a member of the expedition erroneously called John P. in the Biddle text (1:255).

IBEX CREEK
A. Little Muddy Creek, entering the MR from n. in Roosevelt Co.
B. Muddy River (Raynolds, 1868); Little Muddy River (Stevens, 1855; Warren, 1857).
See the comment under Argalia Creek.

IBEX ISLAND
A. An island near the mouth of Cow Creek, Blaine Co.

IBEX RIVER
A. Ibex River on Clark's field map (Moulton, pl. 112), but Argalia R. in the Biddle text.
B. Argalia River (Carey, 1814; Burr, 1839).
Clark added the name over an erasure in the text, and added it also to the course and distance record.

INDIAN FORT CREEK
A. Nickwall Creek, entering the MR from s. in Roosevelt Co. Reportedly named for Nick Wall, an Upper Missouri steamboatman (MPNI).

JEFFERSON RIVER
A. One of the Three Forks of the MR. Today the name applies to that segment of the explorers' Jefferson R. extending from Twin Bridges to the Three Forks. Above that point, to Clark Canyon Dam, it is now called Beaverhead River.

JUDITH'S RIVER
A. Judith River, entering the MR from s. in Fergus Co.
B. No other name in general use.
At first this stream was named Big Horn River, because Lewis noted

"great abundance of the Argalia or Bighorned animals" (Thwaites, 2:92). But later in the same entry he wrote, "Cap C. who assended the R. much higher than I did has thought proper to call it *Judieths* River." As Clark himself calls it the Big Horn in his own entry for the day, and on his field map (Moulton, pl. 52), the name Judith may not have been chosen until later. Ordway has no name for the stream at all. Judith or Julia Hancock was the young girl whom Clark had met in Fincastle, Va., and would marry in 1808.

LABICHE'S RIVER

A. Sarpy Creek, entering the YS from s. in Treasure Co.

B. Labeich River (Warren, 1855).

Named for Pvt. Francis Labiche, a member of the expedition. In Thwaites, 5:302, the words *"I call R. Labeech"* were added later in Clark's hand. In the 1850s, John B. Sarpy of the American Fur Company built two posts on the Yellowstone, the first just below the mouth of the Rosebud and the second about twenty-five miles below the mouth of the Big Horn.

LARK RIVER

A. Black Coulee, entering the MR from n. in Blaine Co.

LITTLE BIGHORN RIVER

A. A fork of the Bighorn, charted but not seen by Clark.

B. Little Horn River (Bonneville, 1837; Burr, 1839; Stuart, 1863); Little Big Horn River (Raynolds, 1868); Little Horn Creek, De Lacy, 1865).

Clark at first mistook the Rosebud for the Little Big Horn, and streams with both names appear on his published maps. He was not to receive accurate information about the Little Big Horn until it was given him by George Drouillard, a member of the expedition who again traveled the area as a trader and had returned to St. Louis by September 1808. Notes and a map, in the hands of both Lewis and Clark, with a heading in Lewis's hand reading "Notes on the chart obtained from George Dreulyard September 6th 1808," is reprinted in Skarsten, 338.

LITTLEDOG CREEK

A. Sand Creek, entering the MR from s. in Fergus Co.

LITTLEDRY CREEK
  A. Elk Prairie Creek, entering the MR from s. in McCone Co.

LITTLEDRY RIVER
  A. Prairie Elk Creek, entering the MR from s. in McCone Co.

LITTLE HORN RIVER
  A. Probably Armell's Creek, entering the YS from s. in Rosebud Co.
  B. Charted as Little Horn by Tanner, 1822.

LITTLE WOLF MOUNTAINS
  A. Bull Mountains, Musselshell Co.

LITTLE WOLF RIVER
  A. Great Porcupine River, entering the YS from n. in Rosebud Co.
  B. Little Wolf River (Tanner, 1822; Ferris, 1836; Warren, 1855); Great Porcupine Creek (Raynolds, 1868).
  Little Wolf Mountain River, with no Indian equivalent, was on Clark's list of Yellowstone tributaries made at Fort Mandan in the winter of 1804–5.

MCNEAL'S CREEK
  A. Blacktail Deer Creek, entering the Beaverhead R. from s. in Beaverhead Co.
  Named for Pvt. Hugh McNeal, a member of the expedition.

MADISON RIVER
  A. One of the Three Forks of the MR. See under Three Forks.
  B. Madison's Fork (Stevens, 1855).

MARIA'S RIVER
  A. Marias River, entering the MR from n.w. in Chouteau Co.
  B. Maria's River (Carey, 1814; Tanner, 1822); Marias River (Burr, 1839); Kay-i-you, Bear's, or Maria's River (Stevens, 1855).
  One of the few places we can say was named at the time of discovery by Lewis and Clark, and that has retained the same name without a break. On 8 June 1805, Ordway wrote that the river was to be called Mariah (Ordway, 228). Lewis named it on the same day (Thwaites, 2:10), though his flowery tribute to Miss Maria W——d may have been

added later. Clark used the name Maria in a note for his field map (Moulton, pl. 41). Maria Wood was a distant cousin of Lewis's, being the granddaughter of his uncle Nicholas Lewis.

The Indians had not told Lewis and Clark about the Marias in advance, and some time was spent in determining whether or not it was the main stream of the Missouri. Robert Saindon, of Helena, Montana, suggests that because the Hidatsas' route to the western tribes, as shown on Clark's 1805 map, cuts south of the Marias, this river may not have been known to them.

MARTHA'S RIVER

A. Big Muddy Creek, entering the MR from n. in Roosevelt Co.

B. River du Foin [Hay River] (Evans, 1796, in Nasatir, 498); Martha's River (Carey, 1814; Tanner, 1822); Martin's River (Burr, 1839); Big Muddy River (Warren, 1855, 1857; Raynolds, 1868).

In his 1796 reference to the Rivière du Foin or Hay River (Nasatir, 498), explorer John Evans does not definitively identify it with the present Big Muddy. He calls it "a River that comes from the N.W. and which joins the Missouri near the mouth of the Yellow Stone River . . . a large and fine River in which there is More Beaver and Otters than in any other part of the Continent."

When the expedition came to the river on 29 April 1805, Ordway wrote, "We named it little yellow River" (Ordway, 205). Lewis put the name at the end of his entry for 29 April, "This stream my friend Cap. C. named Marthas river," and wrote and crossed out the words "in honour of Miss M——." But he did not enter it in his course and distance section. Frequently we find a name in the text which is not in the unrevised courses and distances because, once written, the latter data do not need revising while the text can easily be changed and augmented.

On the same day Clark wrote, "We call this river Marthey's river in honor to the Selebrated M.F." The woman, obviously admired by Clark, has not been identified. Clark also omitted the name from his field map and courses and distances for 29 April. We may conclude that the explorers may have considered calling the river the Little Yellow or Little Yellowstone, because of its proximity to the Yellowstone; and that sometime before the expedition returned, it became Marthy's or Marthey's River (Jackson, 1:317). Clark called it Marthys River on his map of 1810, and it became Martha's in the Biddle edition.

MASHASKAP RIVER

The Indians at Fort Mandan gave Clark the name of this stream, and located it as entering the YS from s. between the Big Horn and the Tongue. There is no major stream in that location. Either the whole thing was a misunderstanding, or the stream is Graveyard Creek, which enters the YS from s. in Rosebud Co. Graveyard Creek hardly deserves a place on the map given to Clark by Sheheke (Moulton, pl. 39b). Warren, 1855, shows the Mashaskap.

MEDICINE RIVER

A. Sun River, entering the MR from w. at Great Falls in Cascade Co.

B. Medicine Creek (Tanner, 1822); Medicine or Sun River (Stevens, 1855; Warren, 1857; Raynolds, 1868); Sun River (De Lacy, 1865); Sun or Medicine River (MRC map of 1892-95, sheet 77).

The explorers had been told of the Medicine River by the Hidatsas and were expecting it. On 14 June 1805, Clark speculated that since the Indians called all unaccountable things "medicine," the name may have originated in the mysterious booming noises which they had heard coming from up this river (Thwaites, 2:157).

The gradual change to Sun River is apparent in the names shown on subsequent maps. Today the stream is officially the Sun River. James Doty, secretary to Isaac Stevens, pointed out in 1854 that the Blackfoot names for sun and medicine are similar (MPNI).

MILK RIVER

A. Milk River, same name on all maps inspected, enters the MR from n. in Valley Co.

B. Rivière blanc [White River] (Evans, 1796-97, in Wood and Thiessen, pl. 3 E); Milk River in other sources.

Lewis and Clark had been told that a large northern affluent of the Missouri was "the river which scolds at all others." They assumed this was that stream, though Biddle later speculated that the Marias might have been the one so designated by the Hidatsas. Lewis said they named it the Milk because "the water of this river possesses a peculiar whiteness, being about the colour of a cup of tea with the admixture of a tablespoonful of milk" (Thwaites, 2:10).

MISSOURI RIVER

Recorded here for consistency, but not pertinent to the discussion.

MUDDY CREEK

A. Tullock Creek, entering the Bighorn R. from s. near its confluence with the YS in Treasure Co.

B. Tullock's Creek (Raynolds, 1868). Named for A. J. Tullock, of the American Fur Company, who built Fort Cass on the s. bank of the YS in 1832.

MUSCLESHELL RIVER

A. Musselshell River, entering the MR from s. between Petroleum and Garfield cos.

B. No other names, but the early spelling was usually Muscleshell or Muscle Shell. Lewis and Clark had been told of this stream by the Hidatsas.

NATURAL WALLS. SEE STONE WALLS.

NORTHMOUNTAIN CREEK

A. Rock Creek, entering the MR from n. in Phillips Co.

B. Mountain River (Carey, 1814); North Mountain River (Ferris, 1836; Burr, 1839); Little Rocky Mountain River (Stevens, 1855); Little Rock Mountain Creek (Raynolds, 1868).

Upon reaching this creek, the expedition came in full sight of the Little Rocky Mountains, which Clark had caught a glimpse of a few days earlier.

ONION ISLAND

A. An island now submerged in the waters of Hauser Reservoir in Lewis and Clark Co.

A large field of wild onions was found here, causing Biddle to remark, "It will no doubt be an acquisition to the settlers" (2:433).

ORDWAY'S CREEK

A. Little Prickly Pear Creek, entering the MR from s.w. in Lewis and Clark Co.

B. Name changed by 1855 (Stevens).

Ordway himself did not mention the naming of a stream in his honor. Lewis, who kept the main entry for the day, put it both in text and in course and distance records; Clark, who was away, appears to have added the name to his text later (Thwaites, 2:244, 246, 247.)

OTTER CREEK
  A. Sweet Grass Creek, entering the YS from n. in Sweet Grass Co.
  B. Otter Creek (Ferris, 1836); Otter River (De Lacy, 1865).

PANTHER CREEK
  A. Big Pipestone Creek, entering the Jefferson R. from w. in Jefferson Co.
  B. Pipestone Creek (Coues, 1893).
So named because Pvt. Reubin Field killed a mountain lion at the mouth of the creek (458).

PHILANTHROPY RIVER
  A. Ruby River, entering the Jefferson R. from s.e. in Madison Co.
  B. Philanthropy River (Ferris, 1836); Pah-sam-meri, or Stinking Water (Stuart, 1863); Stinking Water (Coues, 1893). The modern name derives from the rubylike garnets in the stream bed.
  Above the Three Forks the expedition encountered three branches of the Jefferson which they gave fanciful names in honor of the President, as Lewis wrote, "in commemoration of . . . those cardinal virtues, which have so eminently marked that deservedly selibrated character through life" (Thwaites, 2:316). These were the Philosophy, the Philanthropy, and the Wisdom rivers. The American people would make short work of such "uppity" names when settlement began. In short, the names of the main Three Forks have survived because they suited the temperament of the American pioneers, and the three minor ones disappeared because they deserved to do so.
  Stinkwater or Stinking Water were common names in the West for streams with a sulphurous odor.

PHILOSOPHY RIVER
  A. Willow Creek, entering the MR from s. in Gallatin Co. See under Three Forks.

PINE CREEK
  A. A stream mapped by Clark between Werner's and Gibson's creeks, emptying into what is now Fort Peck Reservoir.
  B. Pine Creek (Tanner, 1822; Ferris, 1836).
So named because at this point the explorers saw their first pine trees since leaving the Wood River camp.

PINE ISLAND

A. See Half-Breed Island at Lone Pine or Half-Breed Rapids, (MRC map of 1892–95, sheet 72).

In editing the Biddle edition, Coues (2:418n) said the island was still present—late in the nineteenth century—at the mouth of what he called Sheep Creek.

POMPEY'S PILLAR, POMPEY'S TOWER

A. Pompey's Pillar, a rocky formation on the s. bank of the YS in Yellowstone Co., 28 mi. n.e. of Billings. Called a pillar in the text and a tower on the map, but now officially a pillar.

Clark named the formation Pompy's Tower and described it as being "200 feet high and 400 paces in secumpherance" (Thwaites, 5:292). He said he carved his name and date on the face of the rock—traces of which remain today and are being protected. But Granville Stuart, writing in 1863, noted "the names of Captain Clarke and two of his men" (Stuart, 157). It is clear that Clark named the tower for Sacagawea's small son Jean Baptiste, whom Clark had nicknamed Pomp or Pompy. Biddle, who interviewed Clark in 1810 but appears not to have discussed the reason for the name in his notes (Jackson, 2:497–545), assigned it the name Pompey's Pillar.

PORCUPINE RIVER

A. Poplar River, entering the MR from n. in Roosevelt Co.

B. Porcupine River (Tanner, 1822; Burr, 1839); Poplar River (Stevens, 1855; Warren, 1857); Poplar Creek (Raynolds, 1868).

PORTAGE CREEK

A. Belt Creek, below the Great Falls in Cascade Co.

B. Portage Creek (Ferris, 1836); Belt Mountain Creek (De Lacy, 1865).

To Ordway this was Red Creek on the westward journey and Portage Creek on the return (239, 381). Clark first called it Portage or Red Creek (Moulton, pl. 54):

POTTS' CREEK

A. Prickly Pear Creek, entering the MR from n. at Lake Helena in Lewis and Clark Co.

B. Prickly Pear Creek (Stevens, 1855; Warren, 1857); Big Prickly Pear Creek (Coues, 1893).

Upon seeing a signal fire set by Indians, the captains at first called this stream Smoke Creek. Then Lewis altered his text to Potts Creek and Clark wrote Potts Valley Creek on his field map (Moulton, pl. 62).

PRAIRIE OF THE KNOBS

A. Blackfoot Prairie or Stevens Prairie in Powell Co.

B. Stevens Prairie (Mullan, 1863).

Lewis first called it Knob Plains on 6 July 1806 (Thwaites, 5:191), then substituted "The Prairie of the Knobs." Here is an example of scientific observers knowingly changing Lewis and Clark names despite their avowed claim that they would not. Captain Mullan honors his associate, Isaac Stevens, by changing this name to Stevens Prairie.

PRYOR'S CREEK

A. Mitchell Creek, a stream entering the MR from n. and now obscured by Canyon Ferry Lake, Broadwater Co.

B. Pryor's Creek (Burr, 1839); Pryor's Fork (Warren, 1857); Pryor's River (Raynolds, 1868).

Named for Sgt. Nathaniel Pryor, a member of the expedition.

PRYOR'S CREEK

A. Pryor's Creek, entering the YS from s. in Yellowstone Co.

Clark named this stream Pryor's River after dispatching Sergeant Pryor and a small party from the Yellowstone detachment to carry a message to Hugh Heney, a North West Company employee on the Assiniboine River. By heading out across country on horseback, Pryor became the first to cross this branch of the Yellowstone, and thus its "discoverer." This name has survived not only as a creek but as a mountain range. Antoine Larocque, who was on the Yellowstone before Clark, said the Indians called the stream the Shot Stone (Wood and Thiessen, 1985).

The next day, Clark named a smaller creek for Pryor, entering the Yellowstone from the s.e., but the name did not survive long. It is not on Clark's 1810 manuscript map nor in Biddle.

RATTLESNAKE CLIFFS

A. A rocky formation on the Beaverhead R., Beaverhead Co., about 10 mi. s.w. of Dillon. Locally confused at times with Beaverhead Rock.

B. Rattlesnake Cliffs (Ferris, 1836).

RATTLESNAKE CREEK

A. Rattlesnake Creek, entering the Beaverhead R. from n.w. in Beaverhead Co.

B. Fifteen-mile Creek (Stuart, 1863).

Here is an early instance of the restoration of a Lewis and Clark name. Stuart in 1863 reported that the stream was then called Rattlesnake Creek but had once been called Fifteen-Mile Creek.

RATTLESNAKE MOUNTAIN

A. A southern peak of the Pioneer Mts. in Beaverhead Co.

REDSTONE RIVER

A. Powder River, entering the YS from s. in Prairie Co.

B. Redstone River (Tanner, 1822); Powder River (Burr, 1839; Warren, 1857; Reynolds, 1868).

During the winter with the Mandans, Clark recorded the name Warrahsah or Powder River from Indian information, and Lewis entered the name in material he prepared for shipment to Jefferson. By this time the French and Indians familiar with the river called it the Powder; as French trader Antoine Larocque explained, its fine, powdery sands gave the water a muddy appearance (Wood and Thiessen, 1985).

On the map prepared by the War Department from the draft sent downriver by Clark from Fort Mandan, the name was War-rah-sash or Powder River. But somehow a change had occurred in Clark's translation of the Indian name when he finally reached the mouth of the river during his descent of the Yellowstone in 1806. His field map, surviving only in the O'Fallon tracing, reads "War har sah. red Stone" (Moulton, pl. 120), and his journal entry reads: "the appearance on the hills at a distance on its lower side induced me to call this red Stone river" (Thwaites, 5:310).

The second comprehensive map prepared by the War Department in 1806, based on a Clark original, is of little help because it simply labels the stream "War sar sah" with no translation.

On the large map that Clark prepared after the expedition, generally called the 1810 map, he wrote "War har sah R," again with no translation. But later, and with a coarser pen, he wrote "Powder" for the stream he had first called the Tongue, leaving a Warharsah River intact but still without an English name. This later change must have been made after 1811, when the engraver had returned the manuscript map to him.

In his text Biddle wrote: "Its current throws out great quantities of red stones; which circumstance, with the appearance of the distant hills, induced Captain Clark to call it the Redstone, which he afterward found to be the meaning of its Indian name, Wahasah." Biddle also went back to Clark's field journal and interlined, in red ink, the words "By a coincidence I found the Indian name Wa ha Sah." He may have done this during talks with Clark while he was preparing to write the narrative.

RIVER OF THE ROAD TO THE BUFFALO

A. Blackfoot River, entering the Clark R. from e. in Missoula Co. Lewis and Clark also referred to this stream as Buffalo River and by its Indian name, Cokalahishkit, their version of the Nez Perce name.

B. River of the Road to the Buffalo (Tanner, 1822); Blackfoot River (Ferris, 1836); Big Blackfoot River (Stevens, 1855; Warren, 1857; Mullan, 1863).

RIVERS-ACROSS

A. Boulder River, entering the YS from s., and Big Timber River, entering from n.

B. Upper and Lower Cross Creeks (Bonneville, 1837); Rivers-Across (De Lacy, 1865); Big Boulder River (Bradley, 1876).

ROCHE JAUNE. SEE YELLOWSTONE RIVER.

ROSE RIVER. SEE TANSY RIVER.

ROSE OR ROSEBUD CREEK

A. Rosebud Creek, entering the YS from s. in Stillwater Co.

B. Bush Creek (GLO, 1866); Stillwater Fork (Bradley, 1876); Stillwater River (Coues, 1893).

According to Bradley in 1876 (158), an exchange of names had occurred. Originally the main stream was called Rosebud Creek, and the eastern branch, on which the Crow agency stood, was Stillwater Fork, so called because beaver dams had turned it into pools. But now, Bradley said, the two names had become reversed.

In the Biddle text, the river is "called by the Indians Itchkepipearja, or Rose River" (3:1141), and on the 1814 map it is the Rosebud, not to be confused with the larger Rosebud River downstream (next entry).

ROSEBUD RIVER

   A. Rosebud River, entering the YS from s. in Rosebud Co.

   B. Rosebud River (Tanner, 1822; Warren, 1857; Raynolds, 1860). Often Rose Bud.

So named in the Biddle text and charted on Clark's field map and 1814 published map; probably applied to the wrong stream. See Coues's footnotes (3:1158–59n) for the tangled history of stream names along this stretch of the Yellowstone.

SACAJAWEA OR BIRDWOMAN'S RIVER

   A. Crooked Creek, entering the Musselshell R. from w. in Petroleum Co., a few miles upstream from its junction with the MR.

   B. Sacajawea River (Tanner, 1822; Ferris, 1836).

   In 1979 the U.S. Board on Geographic Names restored the name of this stream to Sacagawea River—the preferred spelling—and abandoned the name Crooked Creek. For uniformity, the board also changed the spelling of Sacajawea Peak, in the Bridger Range 15 mi. n.n.e. of Bozeman, to Sacagawea Peak.

SAMUEL RIVER

   A. Fourmile Creek, entering the YS from w. in Richland Co.

   B. Samuel River (Tanner, 1822; Warren, 1855; De Lacy, 1865).

   The reason for this name in Clark's journal and map is still unknown. On Clark's field map (Moulton, pl. 112), the names Samuel Creek, Ibex Creek, and Buffalo Crossing Creek are written upside down in relation to the other names, as if added later and with a different pen. It does not occur in the manuscript journals, which suggests it was not added until after the expedition.

SCATTERING CREEK

   A. Possibly Burnt Fork, entering the Bitterroot R. from s. in Ravalli Co.

SEAMAN'S CREEK

   A. Monture Creek, entering the Blackfoot R. from n. in Powell Co.

   Called Seaman's Creek by Biddle, and so named on one map drawn by Clark. Named for Seaman, Lewis's Newfoundland dog previously believed to have borne the name Scannon. For an explanation of how the name Scannon became Seaman, see "A Dog Named Scannon—Until Recently" in this volume.

SERVICE-BERRY VALLEY
  A. An area in Beaverhead Valley where the explorers found large quantities of serviceberry (*Amelanchier alnifolia*).

SHANNON'S CREEK
  A. Fly Creek, entering the YS from s. in Yellowstone Co.
  B. Shannon's Creek (Ferris, 1836; Warren, 1855).
  Named for Pvt. George Shannon, a member of the expedition. Originally Clark had Baptist Creek entering the YS from s. and Shannon's Creek from n. (Moulton, pl. 110). He switched these on his 1810 map, perhaps inadvertently.

SHIELDS' RIVER
  A. Highwood Creek, entering the MR from s.e. in Chouteau Co.
  B. Highwood Creek (Stevens, 1860; De Lacy, 1865).
  Named for Pvt. John Shields. Both Ordway and Gass recorded the stream as Strawberry River in their journal entries for 15 June 1805. It appears as Shield's Creek in the course and distance record for that day and on Clark's field map (Moulton, pl. 54).

SHIELDS' RIVER
  A. Shields River, entering the YS from n. in Park Co.
  B. Shields River (Ferris, 1836). Called Twenty-Five Yard River by early traders including Bonneville (1837), and in some treaty documents, but restored to Shields River (Raynolds, 1868, and others). Bradley (152) reported it was still occasionally called Twenty-Five Yard Creek in 1876, but felt the original name should be restored.

SHISHEQUAW MOUNTAIN
  A. Haystack Butte, between the forks of the Sun R. in n.w. Chouteau Co., s.w. of Great Falls.

SHISHEQUAW RIVER
  A. Elk Creek, entering the Sun R. from s. in Chouteau Co. The name was changed from South Fork of the Sun River by action of the U.S. Board on Geographic Names (MPNI).

SHOSHONE COVE
  A. Shoshone or Shoshoni Cove, a mountain cove w. of Clark Canyon Dam, Beaverhead Co.

SLAUGHTER RIVER

    A. Arrow Creek, entering the MR from s. in Fergus Co.

    B. Slaughter River (Tanner, 1822; Ferris, 1836); Arrow River (Stevens, 1855; De Lacy, 1865).

"On the north we passed a precipice about 120 feet high, under which lay scattered the fragments of at least 100 carcasses of buffaloes. . . . These buffaloes had been chased down the precipice in a way very common on the Missouri, by which vast herds are destroyed in a moment" (Biddle, 2:334).

SMITH'S RIVER

    A. Smith River, entering the MR from s. in Cascade Co.

    B. Smith's River (Tanner, 1822; Burr, 1839); Smith's Fork, and Deep or Smith's River (Stevens, 1855); Deep River (Stevens, 1855); Deep Creek (De Lacy, 1865).

Named for Secretary of the Navy Robert Smith.

SNOW MOUNTAINS; SNOWY MOUNTAINS

    A. Big Snowy Mountains, lying mainly in Fergus Co.

    B. Mountain of Eternal Snow (Evans, 1796–97, in Wood and Thiessen, pl. 3 E); Snow Mountains (Warren, 1855).

As Lewis and Clark had access to the Evans map (see Wood and Thiessen), they were not surprised to see these mountains of "eternal snow."

SNOW RIVER

    A. Shonkin Creek, entering the MR from s. below Fort Benton, Chouteau Co.

    B. Snow Creek (Tanner, 1822; Ferris, 1836); Shonkee River (Stevens, 1855); Shonkin Creek (Warren, 1857).

Stranathan suggests that Shonkin is a corruption of the French word *chantier,* or boatyard, and that the cottonwoods at the mouth of the creek were used by French traders in building boats.

SOUTHMOUNTAIN CREEK

    A. Armell's Creek, entering the MR from s. in Fergus Co.

    B. South Mountain Creek (Ferris, 1836).

STICKLODGE CREEK

A. Not positively identified, but see Stick Lodge Creek, entering the MR from s. on the MRC map of 1892–95, sheet 67. Probably today's Hell Creek.

STONEWALL CREEK

A. Eagle Creek, entering the MR from e. in Chouteau Co.

B. Stonewall Creek (Ferris, 1836); Stone Wall River (Burr, 1839).

STONE WALLS; NATURAL WALLS

A. The White Cliffs region of the MR, running from the Judith R. almost to the Marias.

B. Stonewall (Ferris, 1836).

In Ordway's words, "extraordanary walls of a black semented stone which appear to be regularly placed one Stone on the other" (223). Other formations are white, and later European travelers would liken the scene to that of Switzerland and the Rhine Valley. Names such as Citadel Bluff, Cathedral Rock, and Castle Rock would be used. Often called the Missouri Breaks, this section of the river runs more than fifty miles between the mouths of the Judith and the Marias. Lewis called the formation the "Natural Walls."

SULPHUR SPRING

A spring across the MR from Belt Creek at Great Falls, informally called Sacagawea Spring.

TABLE CREEK

A. Little Porcupine Creek, entering the YS from n. in Rosebud Co.

B. Same by 1860 (Raynolds, 1868).

TANSY RIVER

A. Teton River, entering the Marias R. near its confluence with the MR from n. in Chouteau Co.

B. Tansy River (Tanner, 1822); Tansey River (Ferris, 1836; Burr, 1839); Teton or Breast River (Stevens, 1855); Teton River (Warren, 1857; De Lacy, 1865).

Another occasion when Lewis and Clark chose different names for a geographic feature. Lewis was reconnoitering in the area where this stream joins the Marias, and decided to call it the Rose (Thwaites, 2:142). Later, Biddle changed the name in manuscript to Tansey because

Clark had used that name in his journal and map, and seems to have made a better case for the name. Clark mentions on 6 June 1805 that the region abounded in a kind of tansy which the explorers knew well. A domesticated species had been in use since colonial days as a poultice and decoction. The plant, of the genus *Tanacetum,* has fernlike aromatic leaves and small yellow flowers.

The name Teton River appears to date from the railroad surveys of the middle nineteenth century, and may derive from a formation on its headwaters called Teton Butte.

TEAPOT CREEK
A. C K Creek, entering the MR from n. in Phillips Co.
B. Teapot Creek (Ferris, 1836); Kannuck Creek (MRC map of 1892–95, sheet 69).

TEAPOT ISLAND
A. An unidentified island near the mouth of Teapot Creek.

TEN ISLANDS
A. A cluster of islands near the mouth of Whitehouse's or Duck Creek, now submerged by the waters of Canyon Ferry Lake in Broadwater Co.

THOMPSON'S CREEK
A. Birch Creek, entering the MR from n. in Chouteau Co.
B. Thompson's Creek (Ferris, 1836).

THREE FORKS OF THE MISSOURI
Name unchanged since applied by Lewis and Clark, more or less in keeping with the American tendency to use this term for any confluence of three streams (as in northeastern Oklahoma, where the Neosho and Verdigris join the Arkansas). If any names assigned by Lewis and Clark can be considered to have been premeditated, they are the branches of the Three Forks. This was a pivotal geographic location of which they had been apprised by the Hidatsas at Fort Mandan, and the Indian information was surprisingly accurate; the explorers knew within a few miles how far beyond the Great Falls they must travel to reach the forks, and they had the Hidatsas' word that they must follow the most westerly and northerly branch to gain access to what Lewis called the waters of "no other river but the Columbia" (Thwaites, 2:279).

Approaching the forks with this information—still to be verified by their own observations, and the latitude and longitude to be fixed, Lewis and Clark would almost inevitably give the main fork the name of Jefferson. Deciding which of the other two would receive the names of Secretary of State James Madison and Secretary of the Treasury Albert Gallatin must have been a perfunctory exercise. The important naming was that of the Jefferson, and there is little evidence in the maps and journals that any deliberation was required.

THREE-THOUSAND MILE ISLAND
    A. A former island at the mouth of present Carter Creek, entering the Beaverhead R. from s.e. in Beaverhead Co.

TONGUE RIVER
    A. Tongue River, entering the YS from s. in Custer Co.
    B. No other English name found.
Clark had been advised in advance about this river, and was on the lookout for it. In his manuscript journal, "Lazeka or Tongue" appears in bolder pen strokes with signs of erasure, indicating some early indecision.

TOOTH MOUNTAIN
    A. One of the many buttes in Teton and n. Lewis and Clark cos. Coues (2:357) suggests Teton Butte.

TOWER MOUNTAIN
    A. Sweetgrass Hills, near the northern boundary of Toole Co.
    B. Sweet Grass Hills (Stevens, 1855); Three Buttes (Warren, 1857).

TRACK CREEK
    A. Rattlesnake Creek, entering the Beaverhead R. from n.w. in Beaverhead Co.

TRAVELLER'S-REST CREEK
    A. Lolo Creek, entering the Bitterroot R. from w. in Missoula Co.
    B. St. Regis de Borgia (De Smet, 1847); Lou-Lou Creek (Stevens, 1855); Lo Lo Fork (Mullan, 1863).
    The captains assigned this name to the camp where they refreshed themselves on both the westward and eastward journeys, and also to the stream beside the campsite. Like several other names now associated with the expedition, the name Lolo Creek was never used by Lewis and Clark. In the records of David Thompson and of Gen. William H. Ashley,

a Frenchman whose name was spelled Lolo appears several times in the literature of the period. The name appears to have been applied to the stream as early as 1831.

TURF CREEK
   A. Indian Creek, entering the Jefferson R. from e. in Madison Co. just above the mouth of the Ruby R.

TURTLE CREEK
   A. Bullwhacker Creek, entering the MR from n. in Blaine Co.
   B. Turtle Creek (Ferris, 1836); Snake Creek (MRC map of 1892–95, sheet 71).
   C. Clark originally charted the stream as Soft Shell Turtle Creek. He also named a stream Turtle Creek during his descent of the Yellowstone, but the name did not survive the rewriting and publishing process.

TWO-THOUSAND MILE CREEK
   A. Redwater Creek, entering the MR from s. in McCone Co.

WERNER'S CREEK
   A. Clearwater River, entering the Blackfoot R. from n. in Missoula Co.
   B. Werner's Creek (Tanner, 1822); Warners Creek (Ferris, 1836).

WERNER'S RUN
   A. A stream entering the MR from n. in Valley Co., in the Fort Peck Dam impoundment.

WHITE BEARD [BEAR] CREEK
   A. Bear Creek, first s. arm of Fort Peck Reservoir.
   B. White Beard Creek (Tanner, 1822; Ferris, 1836).
   Earlier names applied by Lewis and Clark: No Water Run and Calf Brook.

WHITEBEAR ISLANDS
   A. Whitebear Island, at the head of the Great Falls, Cascade Co.

WHITEHOUSE'S CREEK
   A. Duck Creek, entering Canyon Ferry Lake from e. in Broadwater Co.
   B. Duck Creek (Roberts, 1876).

Named by the explorers for Pvt. Joseph Whitehouse, a member of the expedition.

WILLARD'S CREEK
A. Grasshopper Creek, entering the Beaverhead R. from w. in Beaverhead Co.
B. Grasshopper Creek in De Lacy, 1865, and all maps after gold discovery.

Named for Pvt. Alexander Willard, blacksmith of the expedition. One account says that in 1862, the year of the gold strike in the area, Charles Rumley named the stream Grasshopper Creek because of the great number of such insects found there. When the stream later was identified as the Willard's Creek of Lewis and Clark, the citizens of the new mining town of Bannack were unwilling to rename it because they disliked a fellow townsman named Willard (Sanders, 89).

WINDSOR'S CREEK
A. Cow Creek, entering the MR from n. in Blaine Co.
B. Windsor's Creek (Tanner, 1822; Ferris, 1836).

WINDSOR'S CREEK
A. Muggins Creek, entering the YS from n.w. in Treasure Co.
B. Van Horn's Creek (Coues, 1893).

WINDY ISLAND
A. Unidentified island in the MR a few miles upriver from the mouth of the Musselshell.

WISDOM RIVER
A. Big Hole River, entering the Jefferson R. near Twin Bridges, in Madison Co.
B. Wisdom River (Ferris, 1836; Burr, 1839; Stevens, 1855); Big Hole Fork or Wisdom River (Warren, 1857; Raynolds, 1868); Big Hole River (De Lacy, 1865).

This stream lost its Lewis and Clark name gradually. It narrowly escaped getting a silly name at the start, for Ordway (262) wrote that at first "The North [fork] we call Sensable River because we were Sensable of it." He crossed out that passage, which may only have been a camp rumor. The term Big Hole came with the trappers, as the traditional label for a sheltered wintering place. By 1836 Ferris was still calling the river the Wisdom but the valley was the Big Hole. To Stevens in 1855, the stream running through the Big Hole was the Big Hole Fork or Wisdom River (the present Wise River being the other fork). The name Wisdom survives as a town on the Big Hole River, near the Big Hole National Monument in northwest Beaverhead County.

The name Big Hole may have preceded Ferris's use of Wisdom as the name of the river by decades. British trader John Work used the French name Le Grand Trou, or Big Hole, in his journal of 1831 (see Work) as if it were an established name.

WISER'S CREEK

A. Fourchette Creek, entering Fort Peck Reservoir from n. in Phillips Co.

B. Wiser's Creek (Ferris, 1836; Burr, 1839); Pourchette [Fourchette] Creek (Raynolds, 1868).

WOLF RAPID

A. Wolf Rapids, an area of rapids beginning 6 mi. below the mouth of the Powder R. (Stanley, 1874).

YELLOWSTONE RIVER

A. Yellowstone, joining the MR from s., at the Montana-North Dakota line.

B. Rivière des Roches Jaunes (Truteau, 1796, in Wood and Thiessen, 1985); Rio Amarillo (Spanish map, 1800, in ibid.); Crow or Yellow Rock (Collot, 1804, in ibid.); Yellow Stone (Larocque, 1805, in ibid.).

While variations on the English name Yellowstone have been known since the late 1700s, there is some doubt as to whether the French Roches Jaunes is a faithful translation of the Indian name. Sources as early as Maximilian say that Elk River is the meaning for most Indian names for the stream. In recent years a Crow Indian, Daniel Elk, told a reporter that the French had originally misunderstood the name for Elk River, which sounded similar (*National Geographic*, August 1981, p. 272).

YORK'S DRY FORK

A. Custer Creek, entering the YS from n.w. in Prairie Co.

B. York's Dry River (Warren, 1855); York River (GLO, 1866).

There is room for error in assigning York's Dry Fork the modern name of Custer Creek. Captain William F. Raynolds named a creek in this area after Col. George A. Custer, who had been in an 1873 exploring party which ascended the Yellowstone. But Raynolds said the creek he named was a year-round one, while Clark reported York's Dry Fork as only a "rain drain." For other features named for Clark's servant, see his field map (Moulton, pl. 63), where "Yorks 8 Islands" and "Black Mans Islands" are named.

Notes on Sources

*D*uring three decades I have written of Meriwether Lewis and William Clark as ordinary men performing feats beyond the ordinary; not geniuses, not titans. But my respect for them, and my desire that their work receive the serious attention of historians, geographers, and other scholars, has given my writings a tone that may occasionally have been too academic. Certainly I confess to having thrown at the expedition all the trappings of scholarship, from long bibliographies to footnotes often outweighing text.

After so many years of close association, however, I now find it possible to deal with Lewis and Clark more as friends than as subjects of academic scrutiny. I am comfortable in their presence. The privilege of publishing these essays, some written without reference to journals, scholarly books, or my own yellowing notes, I count as one of the rewards for the dogged pursuit of facts that has marked my earlier writings. Certainly this informal stance accounts for the brevity of the notes that follow.

"At the Mouth of the Yellowstone" reflects my chronic preoccupation with the microcosm. The work done while the explorers were at this location in April 1805 typifies the routines of observing, mapping, journalizing, and military housekeeping that were to preoccupy the men of the expedition for the next year and a half. Only the journal entries of Lewis, Clark, and Ordway are basic here. Paul L. Hedren, superintendent of the Fort Union Trading Post National Historic Site, at Williston, North Dakota, kindly spent a day guiding Catherine and me about that area in September 1985.

To document the speculations in "If the Spanish Had Captured Lewis and Clark," I suppose I would need to review half my library. No particular work strikes me as requiring special notice.

My justification for the very short piece, "Among the Sleeping Giants," is the mental image I carry of Lewis and Clark making their way among those massive, snow-topped cones, as ignorant for the moment as blind men groping at the elephant in the old fable. The task of expanding this little exercise into a longer study of Jefferson's curiously backward views on the value of geology I leave to someone else – including the sheaf of notes that such a study would require.

In "Home to the Unknown" my main source has been the Thwaites edition of the journals, covering the homeward leg of the route.

"William Clark and the Girls on the Pony" deals with the mixed but mostly negative view I hold of the value of family tradition in the study of history. It is largely self-documenting. My belief that the near extinction of the Mandans is traceable to the bureaucratic mediocrity of one man, Secretary of War Cass, is set forth more fully in my *Voyages of the Steamboat Yellow Stone* (New York, 1985), pp. 63–71. Clark's journal of his 1809–10 trip to Washington, including Julia's pickle recipe, is in the archives of the State Historical Society of Missouri.

After I had done the documentary research for "A Dog Named Scannon – Until Recently," Robert and Ruth Lange, of Portland, Oregon, joined Catherine and me in Powell County, Montana, for a pleasurable reconnaissance of the area where Monture Creek joins the Blackfoot. Ernest S. Osgood's original piece on the dog "Scannon" appeared in *Montana, the Magazine of Western History,* Summer 1976. It was reprinted as Publication No. 2, a supplement to *We Proceeded On,* newsletter of the Lewis and Clark Trail Heritage Foundation, Inc.

"Editing the Lewis and Clark Letters" is another self-documented essay, having been drawn from my correspondence file and my recollections.

The final piece in the collection, "Lewis and Clark Place-Names in Montana," is presented with the wish that other students might be encouraged to appreciate the role of place-names in the record of American exploration. The staff of the library at the Montana Historical Society, in Helena, was predictably helpful during my visit there in the summer of 1985. Bob Saindon, of Helena, was generous with his knowledge of the expedition and enabled me to avoid several embarrassments.

The following list of references applies mainly to the place-names essay.

[Biddle, Nicholas]. *History of the Expedition under the Command of Captains Lewis and Clark. . . . Prepared for the Press by Paul Allen, Esq.* 2 vols and map. Philadelphia, 1814. Biddle, who wrote the narrative, did not permit his name to appear on the title page. The 1893 edition, edited in 4 vols. by Elliott Coues, is also cited.

[Bonneville]. A map of the sources of the Colorado, & Big Salt Lake, Platte, Yellow-Stone, Muscle-Shell, Missouri. . . . In Washington Irving, *The Rocky Mountains . . . from the Journal of Captain B. L. E. Bonneville.* Philadelphia,1837.

Bradley, James H. "Journal of the Sioux Campaign of 1876." *Contributions of the Historical Society of Montana*, 2 (1896), 140–228.

Burr, David H. Map of the United States of North America with Parts of the Adjacent Countries. Washington, 1839. Burr was geographer to the House of Representatives and had access, apparently through General William H. Ashley, to a map of Jedediah Smith's travels.

Carey, Matthew. Map of Missouri Territory, formerly Louisiana. Philadelphia, 1814. Engraved by Samuel Lewis, who did the Biddle map of the same year. The Yellowstone is mislabeled "Little Missouri."

Collot, Victor. *A Journey in North America.* 2 vols. Florence, Italy, 1824.

Coues, Elliott. See Biddle.

Criswell, Elijah Harry. *Lewis and Clark: Linguistic Pioneers.* Columbia, Mo., 1940.

De Lacy, W. W. Map of the Territory of Montana, with Portions of the Adjoining Territories, 1865. First map of Montana Territory.

De Smet, P.-J. Nouvelle carte du territoire de L'Oregon. Ghent, 1847.

Ferris, Warren Angus. *Life in the Rockies.* Denver, 1940. A journal and map prepared in 1836 but not published until 1940. Although not available to the public before then, it is useful in showing the geographic knowledge of a seasoned westerner.

Gass, Patrick. *A Journal of the Voyages and Travels of a Corps of Discovery, under the Command of Capt. Lewis and Capt. Clarke.* Pittsburgh, 1807.

[GLO]. U.S. Government Land Office. Map of the United States and Territories. Washington, 1866.

Jackson, Donald, ed. *Letters of the Lewis and Clark Expedition, with Related Documents, 1783–1854.* Second ed., 2 vols. Urbana, Ill., 1978.

Kappler, Charles J., ed. *Indian Affairs; Laws and Treaties.* 2 vols. Washington, 1904.

Larpenteur, Charles. *Forty Years a Fur Trader on the Upper Missouri.* Ed. by Elliott Coues. New York, 1899.

McVickar, Archibald, ed. *History of the Expedition under the Command of Captains Lewis and Clarke.* 2 vols. New York, 1842. An abridgement "by the omission of unimportant details" of the Biddle edition of 1814.

Maximilian, Prince of Wied. *Travels to the Interior of North America.* Vols. 22–24, in *Early Western Travels*, ed. by Reuben Gold Thwaites. Cleveland, 1905.

Moulton, Gary E., ed. *Atlas of the Lewis & Clark Expedition.* Lincoln, Nebr., 1983. First volume of a new edition of the journals of the expedition, issued by the University of Nebraska Press. Text of the journals begins with vol. 2, and three volumes have been issued to date.

Mullan, John. "Report on Construction of a Military Road from Fort Walla-Walla to Fort Benton." Washington, 1863. Senate Ex. Doc. 43, 37 Cong., 3d sess., U.S. serial 1149.

[MPNI]. Montana Historical Society Place-Name Index. A card file maintained at the society's library in Helena, Mont.

Nasatir, A. P., ed. *Before Lewis and Clark.* St. Louis, 1954.

[Ordway]. Quaife, Milo M., ed. *The Journals of Captain Meriwether Lewis and*

Sergeant John Ordway Kept on the Expedition of Western Exploration, 1803-1806. Madison, Wis., 1916.

Osgood, Ernest S., ed. *The Field Notes of Captain William Clark, 1803-1805.* New Haven, Conn., 1964.

Raynolds, William F. "Report of the Exploration of the Yellowstone and Missouri Rivers in 1859-1860." Washington, 1868. Sen. Ex. Doc. 77, 40th Cong., 2d sess., U.S. serial 1317.

Roberts, Thomas P. "The Upper Missouri River." *Contributions of the Historical Society of Montana,* 1 (1876), 206-35.

Russell, Osborne. *Journal of a Trapper,* [1834-43]. Portland, Ore., 1955.

[Sanders, Wilbur F.] "Lewis and Clarke's Expedition." *Contributions of the Historical Society of Montana,* 1 (1876), 88-92.

Skarsten, George. *George Drouillard, Hunter and Interpreter for Lewis and Clark.* Glendale, Calif., 1964.

Stanley, D. S. *Report on the Yellowstone Expedition of 1873.* Washington, 1874.

Stearns, Harold G. *On the Trail with Lewis & Clark in Montana.* Booklet, n.d. Lists Montana campsites with present names.

Stevens, Isaac. *Explorations and Surveys for a Rail Road Route from the Mississippi River to the Pacific Ocean. The Rocky Mountains to Puget Sound.* Washington, 1855. Sen. Ex. Doc. 78, 33rd Cong., 2d sess., U.S. serial 768.

Stranathan, F. E. Newspaper clipping, no place or date, but apparently written in the 1920s, headed "Names Given by Lewis and Clark." Copy in Montana Historical Society Library.

Stuart, Granville [1863]. *Forty Years on the Frontier.* 2 vols. Cleveland, 1925.

Tanner, Henry S. A Map of North America, Constructed According to the Latest Information. Philadelphia, 1822.

Thwaites, Reuben Gold, ed. *Original Journals of the Lewis and Clark Expedition, 1804-1806.* 8 vols. New York, 1905-6.

U.S. Geological Survey. 1 × 2-degree quadrangle maps. Source for current Montana place-names.

Warren, Gouveneur K. Section of a map compiled in the Pacific Railroad Route Office with additions designed to illustrate Lt. Warren's report of military reconnaissances in the Dacota Country, 1855. Senate Ex. Doc. 76, 34th Cong., 1st sess., U.S. serial 822.

——. Map of the United States from the Mississippi to the Pacific Ocean. Washington, 1857.

White, Helen McCann, ed. *Ho! For the Gold Fields.* St. Paul, Minn., 1966. Contains diaries by Fisk, Holmes, and Davy wagon train members traveling across Montana in the 1860s.

Wheat, Carl I., *Mapping the Transmississippi West.* 5 vols. San Francisco, 1958-62.

Wheeler, Olin D. *The Trail of Lewis and Clark, 1804-1904.* 2 vols. New York, 1904.

Wood, W. Raymond, and Thomas D. Thiessen. *Early Fur Trade on the Northern Plains.* Norman, Okla., 1985. Contains journals by Larocque, Thompson, McKenzie, and others.

[Work]. *Journal of John Work.* Ed. by W. S. Lewis and Paul C. Phillips. Cleveland, 1923.

Index